Isaac S Moses

Sabbath School Hymnal

A collection of songs, services and responses for Jewish Sabbath Schools, and

homes

Isaac S Moses

Sabbath School Hymnal

A collection of songs, services and responses for Jewish Sabbath Schools, and homes

ISBN/EAN: 9783337038564

Printed in Europe, USA, Canada, Australia, Japan

Cover: Foto ©Lupo / pixelio.de

More available books at **www.hansebooks.com**

THE

Sabbath School Hymnal

A

Collection of Songs, Services and Responses

FOR

Jewish Sabbath Schools, and Homes

FOURTH REVISED AND ENLARGED EDITION.

ARRANGED AND PUBLISHED BY

I. S. MOSES.

CHICAGO.

THE publication of this hymnal has been undertaken as a service of love. It is intended to bring cheerfulness and devotion into our Sabbath Schools. Our children love to sing ; but there has been no book adequate to the taste and capacity of our Sabbath Schools. The present work offers not only songs for the opening and closing of the school ; it is to supplement the religous and ethical instruction of the class-room. Poetry and melody are more potent agencies to impress the mind of the young with the truths of religion and morality than catechisms and chronological lists of events. The Services added to this book are intended to train our children to take part in divine service, to make them familiar with the chief elements of Jewish worship, and thus prepare the way for congregational singing. Trained choirs will always be necessary in our synagogues; for the highest class of music forms now an indespensible element of our service: but the choir should not usurp the function of the congregation. The simple musical responses in the liturgy proper, and the hymn before the sermon should be sung by those who come to worship God. Let the voices of young and old once more be heard in our synagogues. The melodies selected will all be found singable. Many an old familiar tune will meet the ear. The four special services have been prepared with a view to the growing demand for children's festivals. The Flower Service can be arranged also for the closing, or graduating exercises of the school. The Harvest Service for Thanksgiving Day, the National Service for the Memorial Days of the Republic, and the Hanukkah and Purim Service, require no recomendation ; they will be welcomed by superintendents and schools. To conduct these services properly a thorough preperation is absolutely necessary. Each school or congregation should organize a Choral Society, meeting regularly once a week and not interfering with time allowed for the Sabbath school. Once learned, the songs will be taken up by the children from year to year, almost without further preperation.

A selection of Hebrew responses and hymns, drawn from the compositions of Sulzer and Lewandowski, has been added for the benefit of small congregations whose voluntary choirs are often at a loss as to Jewish music.

The undersigned could not have accomplished his task without the assistance of faithful friends. Sincere thanks are due and are herewith extended to the Rev. James Vila Blake for the free use of all his publications. Many hymns and the arrangement of the services must be credited to the experience, the fine musical and devotional spirit of this noble and unselfish friend.

To the Rev. Charles W. Wendte, and the John Church Co., of Cincinnati, for kind permission to use a number of hymns taken from The Carol, a rich collection of songs.

To Mr. E. Rubovits, owner of the copyright of Otto Lob's Hymnbook, for kind permission to use many of its songs.

To Rev. F. L. Hosmer, for translating for the undersigned the beautiful poem of the late Dr. Leopold Stein, "Oh, Day of God," and for kind permission to make use of his published poems. To Prof. G. Bamberger, for original hymns.

To Mrs. Hannah G. Solomon, for kind permission to make use of the Collection of Jewish Melodies published by the ladies as a souvenier of the World's Parliament.

To Mrs. S. E. Munn for the original compositions Nos. 6 and 53 ; Prof. Wm. Otis Brewster for kind assistance and the composition of No. 141; Prof. Luthkin for the original compositions bearing his name; and, last but not least to the editors of the "Ethical Songs," published by the Leighton Neighboring Guild, London, for kind permission to make use of their collection.

May then this book go forth and awaken the echoes of sweet melody in Jewish Sabbath Schools and homes.

Chicago, March 21, 1894. I. S. MOSES.

INDEX TO SUBJECTS.

Songs of Praise 3-25
Morning and Evening 26-37
Festivals and Seasons 38-78
Patriotic Songs 79-93
Songs of Duty 94-111
Songs for the Primary Classes 112-122
Six Services 123-142
The Flower Service 143-146
The Harvest Service 147-151
The National Service 152-156
Hanukkah and Purim Service 157-163
Responsive Readings 164-175
Hebrew Responses and Hymns 176-191

INDEX TO FIRST LINES.

All are architects of fate, Longfellow 97
Ah! how skillfull grows the hand, Longfellow 104
Arise my Soul, Dr. Gutheim 20
A silvery tide called sunny side, C. Gannett. . 120
Are we sowing 36
Backward looking o'er the past, John Chadwick 52
Be true to every inmost thought 95
Brightly glows the day 116
Come forth and bring your garlands 72
Come ye faithful 71
Days of summer glory 73
Day is breaking, J. V. Blake 28
Father I call on Thee, tr. from Theo. Korner 14
Father our prayer we offer 36
Father see Thy suppliant children, Dr. J. K. Gutheim 44
Father thou hast taught the way, Dr. Gutheim, 74
For the sunshine, Felix Adler 19
Father to Thee we look, Rev. F. L. Hosmer . . 18
Gentle ray of sunlight 24
Gently falls the evening, E. Tozer 27
Give to the wind thy fears, J. G. Whittier . . 40
Great God we sing 62
Go my child thus says the Highest 100
God make my life a little light 117
God made the sun 116
God is always near me 118
God of the mighty hand, Rev. David Levy . . 78
God is near, Dr. I. M. Wise 18
God shall keep thee 77
Had not the Lord, Dr. Jastrow 67
Hallelujah, Dr. Jastrow 68
Harvest festival, J. G. Whittier 74
Happy who in early youth, Dr. M. Jastrow . . 46
Happy who never wanders, Dr. J. Gutheim . 9
Happy ye who learn, Dr. Gutheim 12

Hast thou fathomed 122
Have you heard the golden city, Felix Adler . 108
How blessed is who comes 43
How happy is he born or taught, Sir Henry Wotton 98
Honor to him who freely gives, Whittier . . . 106
Holy, holy, holy, Dr. Gutheim 17
Holy Sabbath rest, Dr. J. K. Gutheim 38
In deep devotion, Dr. M. Jastrow 64
I sing the almighty power of God 114
I will extol Thee, (Ps. 145) 65
I will praise O Lord, Dr. Leopold Stein, transl. by Dr. Jastrow 66
Let our day be glad, Dr. Jastrow 64
Let in light, the holy light 110
Let Israel trust, Penina Moise 67
Let us with a gladsome mind 37
Life is onward 100
Live for something 96
Little drops of water 113
Lord let the swelling anthems rise, Dr. J. K. Gutheim 63
Lord in the morning, (Ps. 5.) 6
Lo! our Fathers tender care, Dr. Gutheim . . 16
Lo! the great sun, James V. Blake 22
Morning awaketh 112
Morning breaketh 28
Morning is coming 112
My Psalm, J. G. Whittier 26
None is like God 115
O! beautiful our country, F. L. Hosmer . . . 80
One by One, A. A. Proctor 96
O! Day of God, Dr. Leopold Stein, translated by F. L. Hosmer 54
O! fill our hearts, Dr. I. M. Wise 4
O! holy joy, Dr. M. Jastrow 48
O! Israel hear, Dr. I. M. Wise 31

INDEX TO FIRST LINES—continued.

O! I would sing	30
A Lord! my God, Dr. Gutheim	14
O Lord! Thy children, Peuina Moise	64
On Sinai's height, Dr. J. K. Gutheim	42
O! sing, J. V. Blake	29
Our Shepherd is the Lord, Dr. M. Jastrow	10
Oh sometimes gleams upon my sight, Whittier	111
O! welcome dear and lovely spring, J. V. Blake	70
On wings of wind, Dr. J. K. Gutheim	50
Pour forth the oil	101
Praise the Lord, tr. from Dr. Leopold Stein, by F. L. Hosmer	40
Praise ye the Lord	49
Praise ye the Lord our King	78
Rouse up to work	103
Say not the law divine	94
Say not they die, Malcolm Quin	109
See the rain is falling	118
See the rivers flowing	122
Sing to the Sovereign, tr. Dr. J. K. Gutheim	3
So here has been dawning, Thos. Carlyle	102
Softly breaks the morn	23
Speak gently	107
Splendors of the morning, Felix Adler	22
Sovereign Lord, tr. Dr. J. K. Gutheim	4
Strew all their graves, Whittier	80
Sweet morn	25
Thou art O God, Thos. Moore	25
The call to duty	94
Thy creative power, O God! Dr. Jastrow	62
To the Father, Dr. M. Jastrow	11
Though faint yet pursuing	12
The future hides in it, Goethe, tr. by Carlyle	105
The Harvest days Tennyson	74
The heavens of heaven	81
The heart it has its own estate	98
The heavens declare	98
Truth is dawning	24
There is many a flower, Dr. Felix Adler	6
This is the day of rest, Dr. I. M. Wise	38
There lies a God, Dr. Gutheim	13
There lies a voice within me	99
The rose is queen among the flowers, F. L. Hosmer	122
The Light pours down	34
To the hills I'll lift mine eyes	42
The season changes, Dr. I. M. Wise	53
The springtide hour	73
The sun goes down	60
The spring has called us	121
The still small voice	119
To Thee we give ourselves, Dr. G. Gottheil	58
To Thee, the Lord	34
'Tis Winter now, Whittier	77
The year is swiftly waning	76
Upward where the stars	35
We plow the fields	75
We meet again	8
We lift our tuneful voices, J. V. Blake	31
When Israel of the Lord, Sir Walter Scott	41
When evening shadows gather	33
When o'er us comes the evening	32
When the stars at set of sun	114
When'er a noble deed is wrought, Longfellow	100
Without beginning, Dr. J. K. Gutheim	51
Who taught the bird	113
When warmer suns	70
Who is like Thee, J. K. Gutheim	98
Who is thy neighbor	104

ADDITIONAL HYMNS.

Be still! be still! for all around,	214
Blessed be he that cometh	217
Blest be Thou, O God of Israel	213
Come, O Sabbath day and bring	208
Gently the twilight hours are nearing	214
God, my King, Thy might confessing	204
Hallelujah!	218
Lord what offering shall we bring	210
Morn in its splendor	211
Oh, let my trembling soul be still	209
One and universal Father	208
One God! one Lord! one mighty King!	203
Our Shepherd is the Lord,	205
Praise the Lord, all ye hosts!	218
Praise the Lord! Praise the Lord	215
Summer suns are glowing	212
The Lord Almighty reigneth	218
The world may change from old to new	216
Thou Lord of life, whose tender care	209
To Thee, my God, whose presence fills	203
Who is like Thee, O Universal Lord!	206
Who is like Thee, O Universal Lord!	207

SABBATH SCHOOL HYMNAL.
Songs of Praise.

No. 1.   **Praise.**

1. Sing to the Sovereign of the skies, To His great name a - lone,
Let winged words of praise arise, To the Almighty's throne.
For He has giv'n His law of light A radiant star to be,
To guide our erring steps aright, For all eternity.

2 Praise be to Thee, who didst command
Thy first-born Israel,
In every clime, in every land,
Thy living truths to tell,

O may they ever be our guide,
And bear us safely o'er
Life's dark and swiftly flowing tide,
Until it flows no more.

No. 2. The Lord Reigns.

1. Sov-'reign Lord, whose scep-tre reigned, Ere yet time its course be-gan; Since cre-a-tion was or-dained, It is guid-ed by His plan.

2 When all things fade and decline,
He abides in majesty;
As He was in power divine,
Is and will He ever be.

3 No beginning and no end—
His is rule and victory;

My Redeemer, Rock and Friend,
My salvation's guaranty.

4 When my lips the Lord extol,
I feel safe in every sphere,
Safe in body and in soul:
God with me—I have no fear.

No. 3. Oh! Fill our Hearts.

1. Oh! fill our hearts, Al-might-y King! With

Oh! Fill our Hearts. Concluded.

2 May we instruction now receive,
With willing heart and mind,
And all Thy laws, O, God, believe,
Who art so just and kind.

3 Who watchest o'er our actions here,
And guardest us from ill,
Oh! teach us humbly to revere,
And bow before Thy will.

No. 4.   In Deep Devotion.

LUTHKIN.

No. 5. Walk Before God.

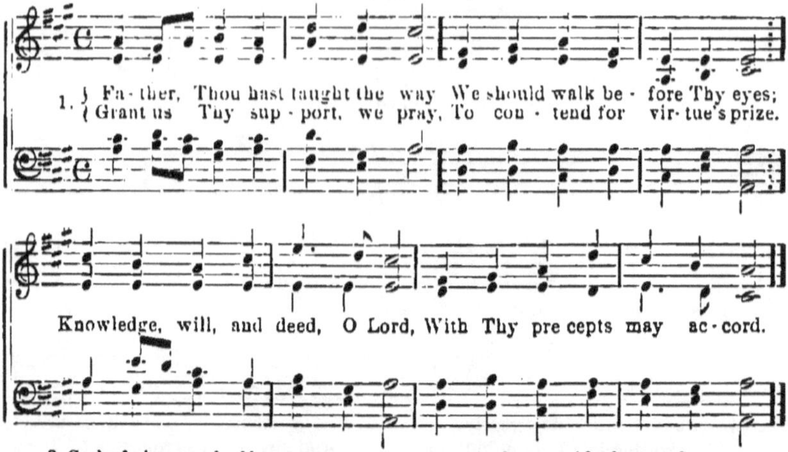

1. { Fa-ther, Thou hast taught the way We should walk be-fore Thy eyes;
   { Grant us Thy sup-port, we pray, To con-tend for vir-tue's prize.
   Knowledge, will, and deed, O Lord, With Thy pre-cepts may ac-cord.

2. God of glory and of love,
   We devote our hearts to Thee;
   Mayest Thou our work approve,
   And our guide forever be.
   Grant that wisdom, virtue, peace,
   Spread and blossom and increase.

No. 6. Truth and Knowledge.

LUTHKIN.

1. There is ma-ny a flower on the path-way of life, The eye of the pil-grim to cheer, But what flow'r is so fragrant, so sweet and so fair, As the flow-er of truth bloom-ing here—

Truth and Knowledge. Concluded.

Here in the gar-den of truth, Here in the gar-den of truth.

2 There is many a treasure, full precious
and bright,
Delighting the heart and the mind,
But what treasure so fair, in its worth to
compare, [find—
With the treasure which here we may
‖:Knowledge, the purest of gold.:‖

3 Then blessed be these halls, where relig-
ion's bright flame
Shines clear and undimmed in its glow;
In the day when we prosper, to guide us
aright,
Our comfort in sorrow and woe—
‖:Here may it dwell evermor.:‖

Second Tune.

{Mrs. S. U. MUNN.

Moderato.

1. There is ma-ny a flower on the path-way of life, The eye of the pil-grim to cheer, But what flow'r is so fra-grant, so sweet or so fair, As the flow'r of truth blooming here— Here, in the gar-den of truth, Here, in the gar-den of truth.

No. 7. We Meet Again.

1. We meet again in gladness, And thankful voices raise;
To God our heav'nly Father, We tune our grateful praise.
His own kind hand hath kept us, Thro' all the changing year,
His love it is that brings us, Again to worship here.

2 We thank Him for the knowledge
   To us imparted here,
  For precept and example
   Laid to our hearts so near.
  For parents dear and loving,
   Our joy and our delight;
  And for our faithful teachers,
   Who make our pathway bright.

3 We thank Him for our country
   The land our fathers trod,
  For liberty of conscience,
   And right to worship God.
  O Lord, our heavenly Father,
   Accept the praise we bring,
  And tune our hearts and voices
   Thy glorious name to sing.

No. 8. The Right Path.

2 In the desert of our wanderings,
　O'er life's wide and trackless sand,
But a single path can lead us
　Safely to the promised land;
But be strong, O man, and doubt not,
　Look aloft, the radiant light
Of the star of truth will guide thee,
　|:In thy troubled course aright.:||

3 O, eternal Father, teach us,
　Well Thy sacred word to know,
Light upon the soul and quiet us,
　On the anxious soul bestow.
May our life be pure before Thee,
　Till its race on earth is o'er,
May Thy blessing rest upon us!
　|:And Thy peace forever more.:||

2 Through night of doom and dread
  We walk, and never tremble;
  By our good Shepherd led,
  We know we shall not stumble.

His light is bliss and health,
  In it we find salvation;
  His comfort is our wealth,
  Be high or low our station.

No. 10. To the Father of all Creatures.

OTTO LOB.

2 Nature round me, sprouting, blooming,
Speaks aloud of life's sweet zest:
Kindles flames of joy, consuming
‖:Every grief within my breast:‖

3 Lord, I praise Thy all-renewing,
Life bestowing power and love,
Thanks and joys, all cares subduing,
‖:Lift my heart all cares above.:‖

Second Tune.

OTTO LOB.

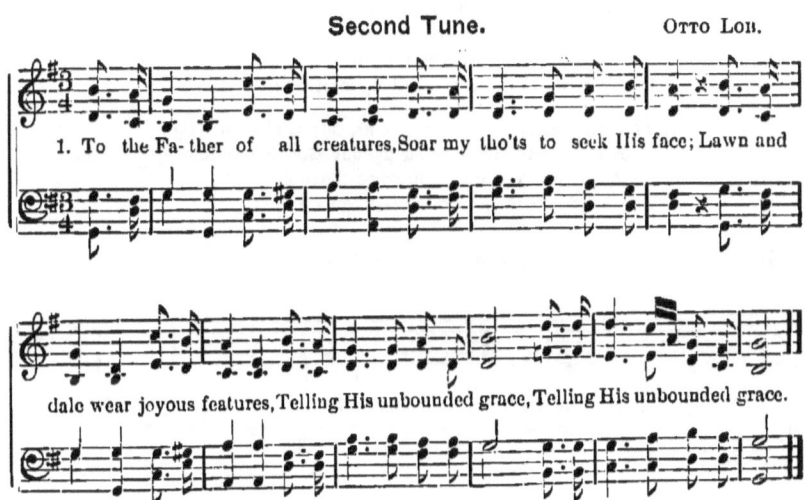

No. 11. Though Faint, yet pursuing.

GERMAN.

1. Tho' faint, yet pur-su-ing, we go on our way, The Lord is our lead-er, His word is our stay; Though suf-f'ring and sor-row and tri-als be near, The Lord is our ref-uge, and whom can we fear

2 He raiseth the fallen, he cheereth the faint,
The weak and oppressed—He will hear their complaint;
The way may be weary, and thorny the road,
But how can we falter?—our help is in God!

3 Though clouds may surround us, our God is our light;
Though storms rage around us, our God is our might;
So, faint, yet pursuing, still onward we go;
The Lord is our Leader, no fear can we know!

No. 12. Happy ye who Learn.

GERMAN.

1. Hap-py ye who learn the teachings Of the Lord in guile-less youth;

Happy ye who Learn. Concluded.

Lof-ty are the young soul's reachings, And her aim is liv-ing truth.

2 Happy fields that in good season,
Have received a holy seed;
Happy ye, whose youthful reason
Has conceived a holy creed.

3 These Thy children, Father, heed them,
Be their trust and staff of life;
On the path of virtue lead them,
Through this world with dangers rife.

No. 13. There Lives a God!

OTTO LOB.

1. There lives a God! each fi-nite creature proclaims His great and wondrous reign.

Thro'out all chang-ing forms of na-ture, His rul-ing hand is clear and plain;

The u-ni-ver-sal ech-oes call, The Lord of Hosts cre-at-ed all.

2 There lives a God! tho' storms are hieing
Athwart the pilgrim's path in life,
The storms are sent for purifying,
And nature smiles beyond the strife.
I, therefore, on my way proceed,
With constant faith in God's kind lead.

3 There lives a God! when life is waning,
His love is near, my soul to save,
My joys are all of His ordaining,
My chast'ning griefs He wisely gave;
In death there blooms new life for me.
God lives! O God, I live in Thee!

No. 14. Father, I Call on Thee.

GERMAN.

1. Father, I call on Thee! Dangers un-numbered hourly expect me; Lord, in Thy mercy, Thou wilt protect me; God of creation, I call on Thee; Father, O guide Thou me!

2 Father, O, guide Thou me!
Guide me thro' life; in death also guide me;
Lord, to Thy mercy I will confide me,
Lord, as Thou wilt, so guide Thou me;
Father, O bless Thou me!

3 Father, O bless Thou me!
Thine is my life, Lord, Thou didst awake it,
Thou who hast given, Thou may'st take it;
In life or death, Lord, bless Thou me,
Father, I worship Thee!

No. 15. Be Thou my Guide.

MENDELSSOHN.

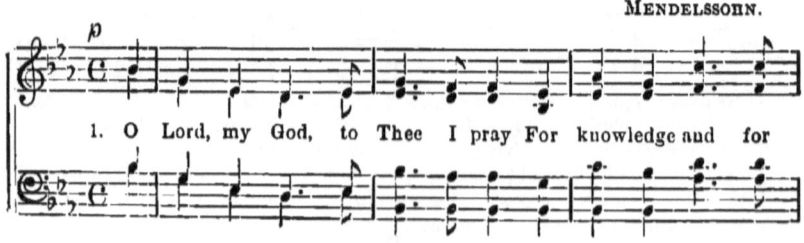

1. O Lord, my God, to Thee I pray For knowledge and for

Be Thou my Guide. Concluded.

2 O shed Thy light into my soul,
   That I may understand
To reach salvation's happy goal,
   Directed by Thy hand.

Each duty be my fond delight,
My courage true, to do the right,
In weal or woe, in joy or pain,
Let hope and faith my heart sustain.

No. 16. Our Guardian Slumbers Not.

OTTO LOB.

1. Lo! our Father's tender care Slumbers not, nor sleepeth;
Gracious gifts His lavish hand Daily on us heapeth.
Tho' fierce storms, tho' perils lower— Is not God our sheltering tower?
Tremble not. At His word the storm is still, Perils vanish at His will— And His love ordains our lot; Lo! our Guardian slumbers not!

2 Lo! our Father's gracious love
Slumbers not, nor sleepeth.
Trust with all thy heart in Him,
Who thy portion keepeth;
Who till now protection granted,
And thy fortunes wisely planted;
Fear thou not!
God, who life and being grants,
Kindly, too, supplies your wants;
Let but duty guide our lot;
Lo! our Guardian slumbers not!

No. 17. Holiness.

1. Holy! holy! holy! God! Lord Eternal, Zebaoth!— Over stars enthroned on high, Over praises' melody, Over all created space, Shine His glory and His grace. Amen.

2 Glorious His rule and might!
Glorious in shade and light!
In the heav'nly blessed choirs,
That His living breath inspires;
Great and glorious is the Lord,
Glorified in every word.

3 Everlasting, unity,
God in sovereign majesty!
Time may change, may swiftly roll,
Firm, unshaken His control,
Now as ever through the past,
To the end of ends will last,

No. 18. Father, to Thee we Look.

P. C. LUTKIN.

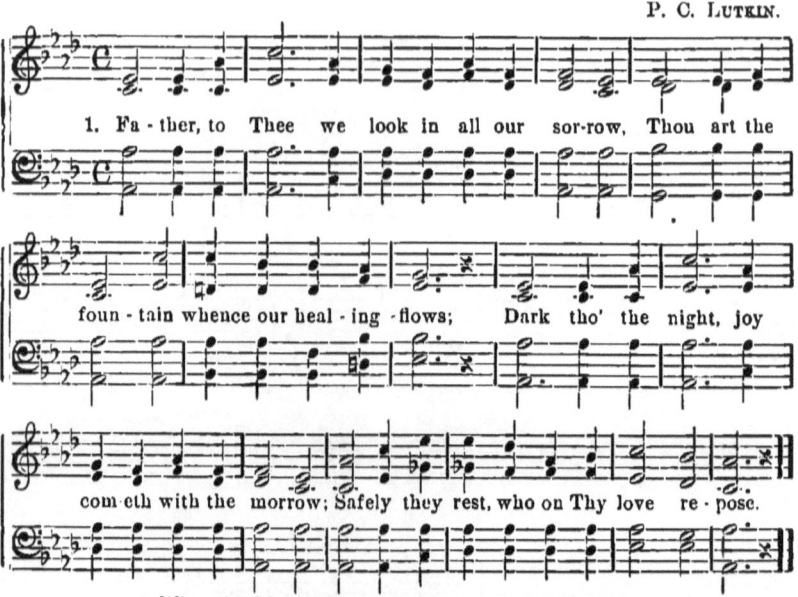

1. Father, to Thee we look in all our sorrow, Thou art the fountain whence our healing flows; Dark tho' the night, joy cometh with the morrow; Safely they rest, who on Thy love repose.

2 When fond hopes fail, and skies are dark before us,
When the vain cares that vex our life increase,
Comes with its calm the thought that Thou art o'er us,
And we grow quiet, folded in Thy peace.

3 Naught shall affright us, on Thy goodness leaning,
Low in the heart faith singeth still her song;
Chastened by pains, we learn life's deeper meaning,
And in our weakness, Thou dost make us strong.

4 Patient, O heart, though heavy be thy sorrows,
Be not cast down, disquieted in vain!
Yet shalt thou praise Him, when these darkened furrows,
Where now He plougheth, wave with golden grain.

No. 19. God Is Near.

LUTKIN.

1. Hear, O Israel, hear; God, thy Lord, is near,

God Is Near. Concluded.

Love and Mer-cy mark His trace; Light from Ser-aph flame,
Truth the an-gels claim. Pours on thee His boundless grace.

2 Sing, O Israel, sing,
God is Lord and King;
He redeems, besides Him none

Suns and stars proclaim
God's exalted name,
One is He, Eternal One.

No. 20. Thanksgiving.

G. BAMBERGER.

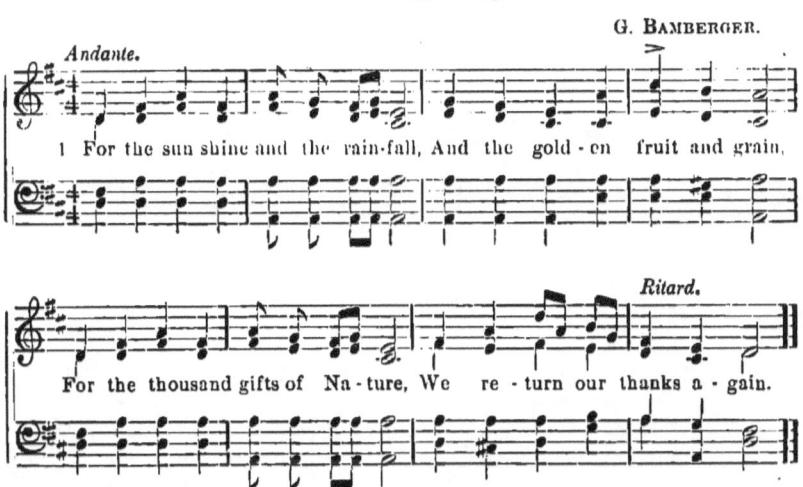

1 For the sun shine and the rain-fall, And the gold-en fruit and grain,
For the thousand gifts of Na-ture, We re-turn our thanks a-gain.

2 For our parents and our teachers
They the patient and the wise,
Who enrich our minds with knowledge,
All our hearts in thanks arise.

3 We give thanks, and we will pay them
With our future deeds on earth,
We will show our grateful feelings
By our lives of nobler worth.

No. 21 The Law Our Guide.

Otto Lob.

1. Arise, my soul, and wing thee Up to thy Father's throne.
My lips shall sing His praises, And make His mercies known.
Thro' Moses He hath given To us His law, a guide,
That leadeth thro' life's journey All who in it abide.

2 I praise Thee, Lord, I praise Thee,
Thou hast to us unfurled
A light, that made Thy people
A blessing to the world.

My helper in all dangers,
My trust in care and death;
A priest I will be ever,
Of Israel's holy faith.

2 The One is He!
To that sole God alone do cling,
Him let no doubt or error from thee wring;
 And tho' temptations press on thee,
Cleave fast to Him, and never yield;
He will protect thee by thy shield;
 O, hear, hear, Israel!

3 Eternal stands
His love, the world His boundless grace
Entwines, as with a Father's kind embrace,
 And to all time His love expands.
Then firmly guard His law alone,
The Lord, our God, the Lord is One:
 O, hear, hear, Israel!

No. 23. Morning Song.

G. BAMBERGER.

1. Splen-dor of the morn-ing sun-light, Shine in-to my heart to-day, Flood each cran-ny of my be-ing, With new strength and spir-it gay, With new strength and spir-it gay.

2. Let me use the golden hours,
   As they glide so swiftly by;
   Freight them with a precious freight of
   ‖:Truth and love and knowledge high.:‖

3. Let me prompt be in my duties,
   Earnest to improve my mind;
   Grateful to my guides and teachers,
   ‖:And to all my comrades kind.:‖

4. And when evening comes, and twinkling
   Stars my conduct seem to ask,
   May I look aloft and tell them
   ‖:I have finished well my task.:‖

No. 24. Holy and Beautiful Day.

GERMAN.

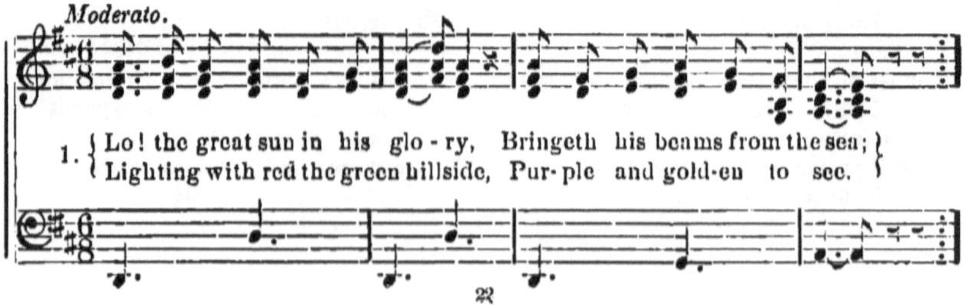

1. { Lo! the great sun in his glo-ry, Bringeth his beams from the sea;
     Lighting with red the green hillside, Pur-ple and gold-en to see. }

Holy and Beautiful Day. Concluded.

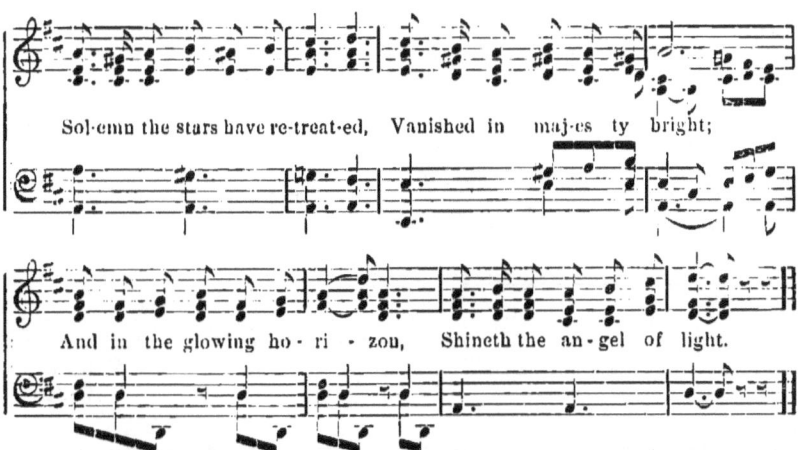

2 Sweetly with songs do we greet thee,
Holy and beautiful day;
Cheerfully, joyfully greet thee,
Singing our youth's happy lay.

Stay with us, stay with our bright band,
Where there is singing and joy,
Let not too quickly the sweet hours,
Our happy meeting destroy.

No. 25. Softly Breaks the Morning.

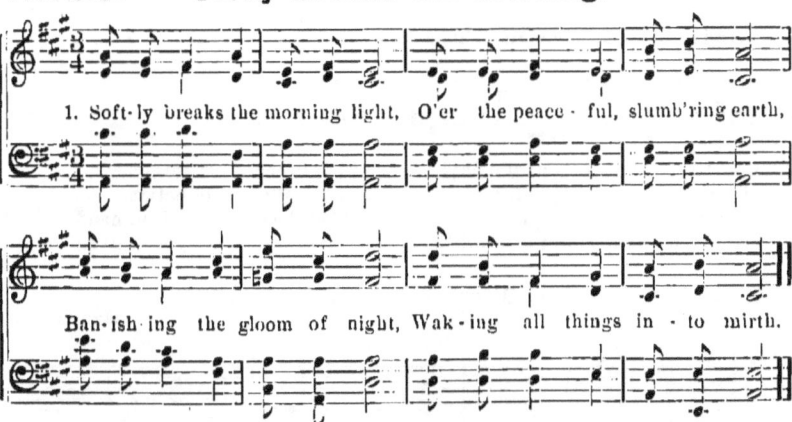

2 Rosy beams illume the hills,
Then, descending, valleys glow;
Now no cloud of darkness fills
Any spot of earth below.

3 Thus the truth in silent pow'r
Dawns upon the human brain,

Touching first the heights that tow'r,
Then, expanding, floods the plain:

4 Mental heights all bathed in love,
Earnest hearts that will not rest,
Until vale and darkened grove
Shine, with daylight's glory blest.

No. 26. The Dayspring.

Adagio.

1. Truth is dawn-ing! see the morning Kin-dled o - - ver sea and land!
   And the gild-ed hills are warning That the day - - spring is at hand!
   Far a-down it flows and brightens, And the dis-tant mountain lightens, With the day - spring near at hand.

2 Brothers, onward! lo! our standard,
  Soaring in immortal youth!
  Trustful ever, fearful never,
  Girded with the might of Truth!

  Listen to the acclamation,
  Nation calling unto nation,
  That the dayspring is at hand,
  That the dayspring is at hand.

No. 27 He Makes His Sun to Rise.

GERMAN.

Andante.

1. Gen-tle ray of sun-light gleaming From 'the por - tals of the sky,
   With ce-les - tial glo - ry beaming, Full of light and life and joy;

He Makes His Sun to Rise. Concluded.

gild-ing ev-'ry hill and mountain, Smiling on their rug-ged side, Cheering ev-'ry crys-tal fountain, While its spark-ling wa-ters glide.

2 Like to Thine is love's sweet mission,
On life's daily path to shine;
Us to give a happy vision,
Of still brighter rays divine:

Love will soothe the sick man's pillow,
Love will light the poor man's day,
Love will gild time's rolling billow,
As it bears us on our way.

No. 28.   Sweet Morn.

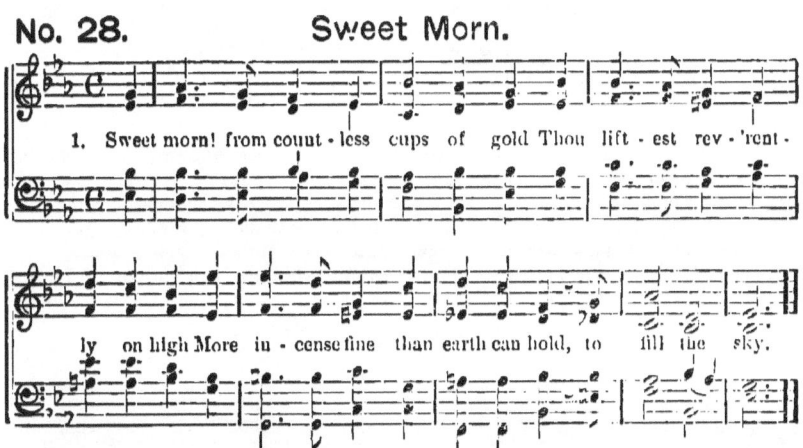

1. Sweet morn! from count-less cups of gold Thou lift-est rev-'rent-ly on high More in-cense fine than earth can hold, to fill the sky.

2 Where'er the vision bound'ries glance
Existence swells with living pow'r,
And all th'illumined earth's expanse
Inhales the hour.

3 In man, O morn! a loftier good
With conscious blessing fills the soul,
A life by reason understood,
Which metes the whole.

4 To thousand tasks of fruitful hope,
With skill against his toil he bends,
And finds his work's determined scope
Where'er he wends.

5 From self, and selfish toil and strife,
To glorious aims his soul may rise;
Each dawn may wake to better life.
With purer eyes.

No. 29. Thou Art, O God, the Life and Light.

2 When day, with farewell beam, delays
  Among the opening clouds of even,
  And we can almost think we gaze
  Through golden vistas into heaven,—
  Those hues, that make the sun's decline
  So soft, so radiant, Lord, are Thine.

3 When youthful spring around us breathes,
  Thy spirit warms her fragrant sigh;
  And ev'ry flow'r the summer wreathes
  Is born beneath Thy kindling eye:
  Where'er we turn, Thy glories shine,
  And all things fair and bright are Thine

No. 30. My Psalm.

My Psalm. Concluded.

The win-dows of my soul I throw wide o-pen to the sun.

2 No longer forward or behind,
  I look in hope or fear,
But, grateful, take the good I find,
  The best of now and here.

3 All as God wills, who wisely heeds,
  To give or to withold;
And knoweth more of all my needs
  Than all my prayers have told.

4 Enough that blessing understood
  Have marked my erring track;—
That wheresoe'er my feet have swerved,
  His chastening turned me back;—

5 That more and more a Providence
  Of love is understood,
Making the springs of time and sense
  Sweet with eternal good.

No. 31. Gently Falls the Evening.

1. Gently falls the ev-'ning shadows O'er the hills and o'er the plains, Cattle slumber in the meadows, Hushed are now the wild bird's strains.

2 Whisp'ring leaves in light winds quiver,
  Moonbeams flush the silent grove,
Stars gleam on the brimming river,
  Earth is wrapped in folds of love.

3 Have we in the day just going [high,
  Breathed pure thoughts and purpose

Used the hours now past us flowing
  Wisely, ere the night draws nigh?

4 On our hearts sweet peace is falling
  Softly, like the shades of night,
And to each a voice is calling,
  "Be thou faithful to the right."

No. 32. Day is Breaking.

GERMAN.

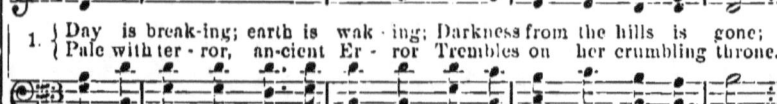

1. Day is break-ing; earth is wak-ing; Darkness from the hills is gone;
Pale with ter-ror, an-cient Er-ror Trembles on her crumbling throne.

Up to la-bor, friend and neighbor! Hope, and work with all thy might;

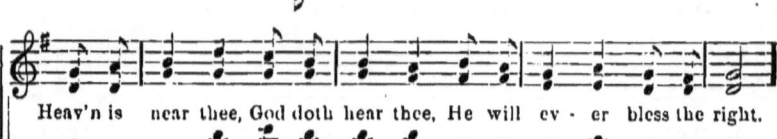

Heav'n is near thee, God doth hear thee, He will ev-er bless the right.

2 Day is breaking, earth is waking;
Fellow-worker, lend thine ear;
Hear'st thou not the angel speaking
Words of love and words of cheer?

Then to labor, friend and neighbor,
Cheerfully put forth thy might;
Never fear thee, God is near thee,
He doth ever bless the right.

No. 33. Aspiration.

1. Morn-ing break-eth on thee, Fresh life's pul-ses beat,

Earth and sky new-kin-dled Once a-gain to greet;

Aspiration. Concluded.

2 Day is all before thee,
   Vanished is the night;
   Wouldst thou aught accomplish—
   Look toward the light;
   Let a mighty purpose
   In thee stir and live,
   After highest being
   Ever more to strive.

3 As thro' mist and vapour
   Breaks the morning sun,
   Shine and work, thou spirit,
   Till thy task is done:
   When from farthest hilltop
   Fades the fire of day,
   Best in blessing others
   Shalt thou pass away.

No. 34. Voices of the Prophets.

GERMAN.

2 They came, the Lord's anointed ones,
   In ev'ry age and shore,
   And ever blessed tidings brought,
   And holy witness bore.
   Witness of Love's celestial light,
   Of duty and eternal Right.

3 O thanks that all the ages down,
   The same love is outpoured!
   O thanks, that ev'ry prophet-voice,
   Proclaims one truth, one Lord!
   O holy throng! ye show the store
   Of endless life from more to more.

No. 35. A Song of Praise.

2 Oh! I would sing a song praise,
　Sweet as breathing flowers
　That ope to greet the earlier hours,
　　Never ending
　　Incense sending
　Up, to bless their parent rays—
　So should wake my song of praise.

3 Oh! I would sing a song of praise,
　Holy as the night,
　When heav'n comes to us in the light.
　　Of stars, whose gleaming,
　　Influence streaming,
　Draws us upward while we gaze—
　So should rise my song of praise.

No. 36. We Lift our Tuneful Voices.

GERMAN.

2 And ye who join the swelling lay,
   Sweet melodies employ,
   To help us on our upward way,
   And praises blend with joy.
   We own the tender constant care

That guards us from above;
Let smiles in ev'ry face reflect
The heav'nly light of love,
Let smiles in ev'ry face reflect
The heav'nly light of love.

No. 37. Evening Prayer.

Moderato. GERMAN.

1. When o'er us comes the eve-ning, And sun-light fades a-way, And gold-en clouds of glo-ry Pro-claim the close of day, Then sing we our thanks-giv-ing, To Him who rules a-bove; Who fills the world with beau-ty, And gov-erns all with love.

Symphony.

2 He made the glorious sunlight,
And set the moon on high;
He gave each star its pathway
To wander through the sky.
He bids the day to vanish,
And says, "Let evening be!"
And changeth light to darkness,—
The Lord of Hosts is He.

3 O God, be pleased to guard us
Throughout the silent night,
And raise again our spirits
To wake to morning light.
And spread around our pillow
The curtain of Thy peace;
For Thou dost keep us always,
With love that ne'er shall cease.

No. 38. When Evening Shadows Gather.

ARTHUR S. SULLIVAN.

2 We know not when we slumber,
   That we shall e'er awake,
   To see another day begin,
   Another dawning break;
   But Thou art ever watching,
   Thou wilt our vigils keep,
   And, trusting in Thy mercy,
   We sink in peaceful sleep.

From "The Carol" by per. of The John Church Co.

No. 39. The Light From Heaven.

1. The light pours down from heav-en, And en-ters where it may.
The eyes of all earth's chil-dren Are cheer'd with one bright day.

REFRAIN.
O hear us! O hear us! And give us light di-vine
With ev-'ry need-ed bless-ing, That we may all be Thine.

2 So let the mind's true sunshine
Be spread o'er earth as free,
And fill men's waiting spirits
As waters fill the sea.
REF.

3 Then let each human spirit,
Enjoy the vision bright;
The Truth which comes from heaven
Shall spread like heaven's own light.
REF.

From "The Carol" by per. of The John Church Co.

No. 40. Close of Worship.

1 To Thee, the Lord Almighty,
Our noblest praise we give,
Who all things hast created,
And blessest all that live;

2 Whose goodness never failing,
Through countless ages gone,
For ever and for ever,
Shall still keep shining on.

No. 41. Upward, Where the Stars Are Burning,

W. A. MOZART.

1. Up-ward, where the stars are burn-ing, Si-lent, si-lent, in their turn-ing Round the nev-er-chang-ing pole; Up-ward, where the sky is bright-est; Up-ward, where the blue is light-est,— Lift I now my long-ing soul, Lift I now my long-ing soul.

2 Far above that arch of gladness,
Far beyond those clouds of sadness,
Are the many mansions fair·
Far from pain and sin and folly,
In that palace of the holy,
‖:I would find my mansion there.:‖

3 Blessing, honor, without measure,
Health and riches, earthly treasure,
Lay we at His altar down;
Poor the praise that now we render;
Loud shall be our voices yonder
‖:When we meet before His throne.:‖

From "The Carol" by per. of The John Church Co.

No. 42.   The Prayer of Life.
Andantino.   DUTCH.

1. Father, our prayer we offer; Not ease we ask of Thee,
But strength that we may ev-er Live on cour-age-ous-ly.

CHORUS.
Vic-to-ri-ous and glo-ri-ous The faith-ful life shall ev-er be!
Vic-to-ri-ous and glo-ri-ous, Thy truth shall ev-er be,

2 Not always in green pastures,
  We ask our way to be,
  But steep and rugged pathways
  To tread rejoicingly.
3 Not always by still waters,
  We would in quiet stay,

But smile the living fountains
From rocks along our way.
4 Give strength in hours of weakness,
  In wandering be our Guide,
  In trial, failure, danger,
  O be Thou at our side,

No. 43.   Sowing and Reaping,
Andantino.   FRENCH.

1. Are we sow-ing seeds of kind-ness? They shall blos-som bright ere long.

Sowing and Reaping. Concluded.

Are we sow-ing seeds of dis-cord? They shall rip-en in-to wrong.

Are we sow-ing seeds of hon-or? They shall bring forth gold-en grain.

Are we sow-ing seeds of falsehood? We shall yet reap bit-ter pain.

2 We can never be too careful
What the seed our hands shall sow;
Love for love is sure to ripen,
Hate for hate is sure to grow.

Seeds of good or ill we scatter,
Heedlessly along our way;
But a glad or grievous fruitage
Waits us at the harvest day.

No. 44. Let us with a Gladsome Mind. F. Silcher.

1 & 4. Let us with a glad-some mind, Praise the Lord, for He is kind.

For His mer-cies still en-dure, Ev-er faith-ful, ev-er sure.

2 He with all commanding might,
Filled the new-made world with light.
For His mercy shall endure, etc.

3 All His creatures He doth feed,
His full hand supplies their need.
For His mercy shall endure, etc.

Festivals and Seasons.

2 ‖:Adoring, stand I here! :‖
O sacred joy, O sacred thrill!
As when a host of angels, still
‖:And soft, to me draw near. :‖

3 ‖:Through blessings to be blest,:‖
The pious to God's dwelling flock,
And praise aloud their heavenly rock,
‖:This is the day of rest!:‖

The Sabbath. Concluded.

2 ‖:Holy Sabbath-joy!:‖
O! our yearning soul inspire:
Warm us with thy heavenly fire,
That in sacred hyms of praise
We to God our hearts upraise.

3 ‖:Holy Sabbath-peace!:‖
Bid all worldly thoughts retire;
Make our heart a sacred lyre;
Bless this day—preferred by Thee—
Emblem of eternity.

Second Tune.
LUTHKIN.

No. 47. Praise the Lord.
Traditional.

2 Lo! He frees all He sees;
  Trusting in His power
  Doth impart to each heart
  Comfort every hour.
  Threat what may, He is aye
  Our defense and tower.

3 God is here; help is near,
  When the storms are raging:
  "Peace, be still," at His will
  Ceases their wild raging,
  Trust, my heart, on thy part,
  E'er His love engaging.

4 Lo! the spring joy doth bring:
  Winter's frosts are ended;
  Gladness reigns, life remains,
  With sweet pleasure blended,
  God doth bear what His care
  And His love defended.

5 Father, we pray to Thee,
  Let Thy grace be o'er us!
  Let Thy light in our night
  Show Thy paths before us!
  Ours Thy love from above,
  And Thy grace which bore us.

No. 48. Fear Not!

Fear Not! Concluded.

God hears thy sighs and counts thy tears, God shall lift up thy head.

2 Through waves and clouds and storms,
  He gently clears the way;
  Wait thou His time; the darkest night
  Shall end in brightest day.

3 Far, far above thy thought
  His counsel shall appear,
  When fully He the work hath wrought,
  That caused thy needless fear.

No. 49.   The Guide in the Wilderness.

W. KNAPP.

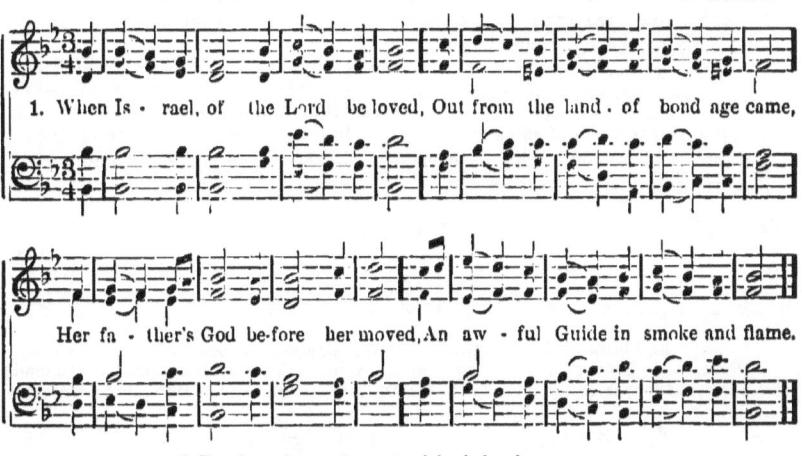

1. When Is-rael, of the Lord be-loved, Out from the land of bond-age came, Her fa-ther's God be-fore her moved, An aw-ful Guide in smoke and flame.

2 By day along the astonished lands
  The cloudy pillar glided slow;
  By night Arabia's crimsoned sands
  Returned the fiery column's glow.

3 Thus present still, though now unseen,
  When brightly shines the prosperous day,
  Be thoughts of Thee a cloudy screen,
  To temper the deceitful ray!

4 And O! when gathers on our path
  In shade and storm the frequent night,
  Be Thou, long suffering, slow to wrath,
  A burning and a shining light.

NO. 50.   On Sinai's Height.

1. On Sinai's height a spring is welling, Which pours its flood in circles wide,
Its crystal stream is ever swelling, And fraught with blessings in its tide.
Its waters joy and strength impart, To ev'ry faithful, thirsting heart.

2 On Sinai's crest a tree is growing;
　A tree of life, with wide spread arms,
No words however strong and glowing,
　Can fitly paint its glorious charms,
To all who garner its increase
This tree yields happiness and peace.

3 On Sinai shines a sun of splendor,
　From which a flood of glory streams:
Its rays delight in hearts engender;
　And rapture sweet its heav'nly beams;
Whose eye is kindled by its light
Will ever walk the path of right.

4 The law which God to us has granted
Is *Spring* and *Tree* and *Sun* combined;
By it eternal life was planted
In souls which are to truth inclined;
All, who its precepts know and guard,
From man have praise, from God reward.

No. 51.   Guide.

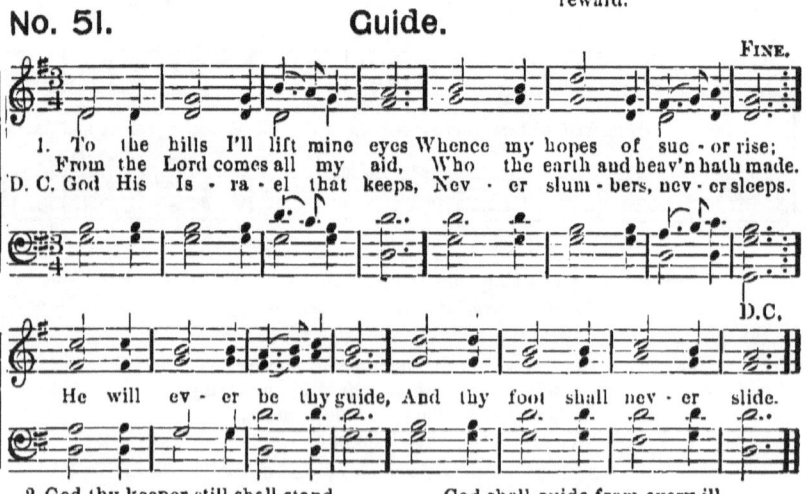

1. To the hills I'll lift mine eyes Whence my hopes of succor rise;
From the Lord comes all my aid, Who the earth and heav'n hath made.
D.C. God His Israel that keeps, Never slumbers, never sleeps.

He will ever be thy guide, And thy foot shall never slide.

2 God thy keeper still shall stand,
　As a shade on thy right hand;
Neither sun by day shall smite,
Nor the silent moon by night.
God shall guide from every ill,
Keep thy soul in safety still;
Both without and in thy door,
He will keep thee evermore.

No. 52. Blessed be ye who Come!
(Confirmation.)

CHORUS.   OTTO LOB.

No. 53. Father, see Thy Children.

(Confirmation Hymn.)

Mrs. S. E. Munn.

Father, see Thy Children. Concluded.

No. 54. Happy who in Early Youth.

Traditional.

Happy who in Early Youth. Concluded.

No. 55. The Covenant.

OTTO LOB

2 Oh, what a heavenly blessing
Moves over us this hour!
Oh, joy! we are possessing
A new and holier power.
O Father, make us willing
To glorify Thy name,
Through deeds of truth, fulfilling
The law Thou didst proclaim.

No. 56. The Day of Joy.

OTTO LOB.

1. Praise ye the Lord this day, Who strews with flow'rs your way Ex - tol the Lord! This sa - cred day im - parts Joy to our throb - bing hearts; Har - mo - ny in all parts His works re - cord.

2 Happy is our estate,
The Lord our God is great,
And never far.
He thrills with joy our breast,
By Him this day is blest,
Praise Him with holy zest,
Hallelujah!

No. 57. New Year's Day.

OTTO LOB.

1. On wings of wind roll swiftly by The hours, the days, the year; We can-not check, how-e'er we try, The march of time's ca-reer. A fleet-ing shadow is our life, A brief and passing dream; Its labors are but empty strife, its aims not what they seem. Its aims not what they seem.

2 We step, O God with awe and fears,
　Before Thy holy throne;　[tears,
Our thoughts, our deeds, our joys, our
　To Thee, O Lord, are known.
The angel e'en, so pure and bright,
　Cannot endure Thy test;
How, then, can we approach Thy sight,
　‖:Who are by sin opprest?:‖

3 We cannot hide our trespasses,
　And not our deeds rescind;
With contrite heart we do confess,
　"Our Father, we have sinned!"
O God, Thy pardon we implore,
　Remember, we are frail;
Refresh us from Thy mercy's store,
　‖:Assist us, when we fail.:‖

No. 58. The Eternal God.

HENRY CAREY.

2 Thou wast, when yet all void and dark
   The universe in chaos lay.
Thou spok'st—and order made her mark;
   The earth, the sea, the night, the day
The sky were set by Thy decree.
Thou wast, Thou art, wilt ever be!

3 The lustre of Thy mercy's ray
   Sustains the world in love and light;
And though all things should pass away,
   Thou wilt for ever reign in might.
Thy being is eternity:
Thou wast, Thou art, wilt ever be!

No. 59. At the Parting of the Ways.

Arr. from GOTTSCHALK.

1. Back-ward look-ing o'er the past, For-ward, too, with ea-ger gaze, Stand we here to-day, O God, At the part-ing of the ways.

2 Tenderest thoughts our bosoms fill;
Memories all bright and fair
Seem to float on spirit-wings
Downward through the silent air,

3 Hark! through all their music sweet,
Hear you not a voice of cheer?
'Tis the voice of Hope which sings,
"Happy be the coming year!"

No. 60. Hear My Voice.

1. Lord! in the morn-ing Thou shalt hear My voice as-cend-ing high; To Thee will I di-rect my prayer, To Thee lift up mine eye.

2 Thou art a God before whose sight
The wicked shall not stand;
Sinners shall ne'er be Thy delight,
Nor dwell at Thy right hand,

3 But to Thy house will I resort,
To taste Thy mercies there;

I will frequent Thy holy court,
And worship in Thy fear.

4 O may Thy spirit guide my feet,
In ways of righteousness,
Make every path of duty straight,
And plain before my face.

No. 61. The Seasons Change.

1. The seasons change, the years roll on. All creatures come and pass away; Above all change stands God alone: Our soul's support, our Rock and Stay. His grace abounds; His love is near; His goodness leads us through the year.

2 Resound, ye worlds, with song and praise,
　Your Maker's truth proclaim.
Rejoice in Him, and in His grace,
　Ye mortals who adore His name.
His mercy beams refulgent light
On all who do in Him confide.

No. 62. O Day of God.

O Day of God. Continued.

No. 63. To Thee we Give Ourselves.

(Traditional.) Arr. by G. S. Ensel.

To Thee we Give Ourselves. Concluded.

The Sun Goes Down. Concluded.

No. 65. Thy Creative Power.

OTTO LOB.

1. Thy cre-a-tive pow'r, O God, Fruc-ti-fies the bar-ren sod,
Seeds a-bound in the ground, And their germs are veiled from sight,
These spring out, grow and sprout, From the dark-ness in-to light.

2 And Thy goodness doth ordain,
Sunshine mild and tender rain,
That the germ, thrive grow firm,
And abundant fruit may yield,
All around, crops abound,
And rich harvests deck the field.

3 Thus Thy creatures thro' the lands
Prosper, cherished by Thy hands;
Thy love grants all our wants,
With unchanged solicitude,
Hence to Thee offer we
Praise in filial gratitude.

No. 66. With Grateful Hearts
(Tune No. 2.)

1 Great God, we sing that mighty hand,
By which, supported, still we stand,
The opening year Thy mercy shows,
That mercy crowns it till its close.

2 By day, by night, at home, abroad,
Still are we guarded by our God;
By His incessant bounty fed,
By His unerring counsel led.

3 With grateful hearts the past we own;
The future, all to us unknown,
We to Thy guardian care commit,
And, peaceful, leave before Thy feet.

4 In scenes exalted or depressed,
Thou art our joy, and Thou our rest;
Thy goodness all our hopes shall raise;
Adored thro' all our changing days.

No. 66. Thanksgiving.

P. C. Lutkin.

1. Loud let the swelling anthems rise, Let all the nations sing,
To Him who rules above the skies, Unto the Lord, our King!
The sun, at His command, Renewed the barren ground—
Rich harvest decks the land, And plenty smiles around.

2 Praise ye the Lord, proclaim His might,
Who made our fathers free,
Who gave to us a heavenly light.
The sun of liberty.
A prosperous people hails
Its bright and genial ray,
And golden peace prevails
Wide o'er the land to-day.

No. 68.   Dedication.

Arr. from BEETHOVEN.

2 With wondrous might, from tyrant's hand,
Thou didst relieve the gallant band,
The valiant few who cleansed Thy shrine,
And caused once more its lights to shine!

3 We dedicate our lives to Thee,
O may our hearts Thy temples be!
O light within us, from above,
The precious flames of truth and love!

No. 69.   Our Heroes.

Our Heroes. Concluded.

2 Like our heroes firm and daring,
Like the Maccabees of yore,
We will manly stand, declaring,
"Thou art Lord forever more."

3 Thou, our Staff and Stay, wilt brace us,
Through vicissitudes of time,
And Thy clemency will grace us,
Where Thy glory reigns sublime.

No. 70. The Sovereign Power.
HANDEL.

2 Thy tender mercies brightly shine;
  Immortal is Thy pow'r;
Thy love, a beaming ray divine,
  That lights each passing hour.

3 The mem'ry of Thy goodness still
  Shall grateful hearts pervade,

Thy majesty and glory will
  Forever be displayed.

4 The eyes of all shall wait on Thee,
  For perfect are thy ways;
And pious hearts united be,
  O Maker! in Thy praise.

No. 71. My Salvation's Tower.

Maestoso. (Traditional.)

1. I will praise, O Lord, Thy grace, Fountain of all pow-er! Thou'rt in storms my shelt'ring place, My sal-va-tion's tow-er; What if men as-sail me? What if men as-sail me? God, my Lord, Breaks their sword, He will nev-er fail me!

2 Ever when I sighed in night,
   When the world repelled me,
   God led me again to light,
   And His hand upheld me.
   ‖: Darkness oft set round me,—:‖
   He was nigh,
   From on high,
   And His mercy found me.

3 With my army God did side:—
   We, the few and humble,
   Checked the Syrian's furious tide,
   Made the mighty stumble.
   ‖: Heroes young and hoary:‖
   Spilt their blood
   For their God,
   Giving Him the glory.

4 By the glow of cheerful lights,
   Priests, approved in sufferings,
   Came to Zion, new from fights,
   Bringing God their offerings—
   ‖:Father of creation!:‖
   As this night,
   Let joy's light
   Ever crown Thy nation!

No. 72.   God the Shield of Israel.

2 Blest be the Lord, for He conferred
On me His gracious care;
I have escaped them as a bird
That flies the fowler's snare.
The snare is broke, we are set free,
Forever, Lord, I'll hope in Thee.

No. 73.   Israel's Calling.

(Tune 72.)

1 Let Israel trust in God alone,
And in His power confide,
For He is faithful to His word,
If we in Him abide:
His councils must forever stand,
All nations bow to His command.

2 Let Israel strive for truth alone,
In love to bless mankind,
And in the bonds of brotherhood
All nations soon to bind,
So that they all, with one accord,
Acknowledge and obey the Lord.

No. 74. Hallelujah!
(Anthem.)

OTTO LOB.

Hallelujah! Concluded.

2 ‖:Hallelujah!:‖
Who dare with God our Lord compare?
A helper in distress and care,
   From age to age the same.
He lends the pious strength and trust,
While wicked arms are crushed to dust,
   ‖:Th'Eternal is His name!:‖
      ‖:Hallelujah!:‖

No. 75. Spring Song.

GERMAN.

2 The nightingale and sweet lark sing,
The beetle chirps, the lambkins spring;
On great and small, and man and child,
Falls warm and bright, the sunbeam mild.

3 How free is every living thing,
The bird that spreads his airy wing,
And I who sit on grassy mound,
Where joyful songs of birds resound.

4 What splendor fills the world below!
How great the Lord who made it so!
And here, and far as space may be,
It tells its Maker's majesty.

5 To Him I consecrate my joy!
And pleasures sweet, my thanks employ,
To Him who fills the world with light,
And makes this time so fair and bright.

No. 76. Hymn of Spring.

GERMAN AIR.

Hymn of Spring. Concluded.

2 Earth with her thousand voices sings
  Her song of gladsome praise;
  |:And every blade of grass that springs,:|
  God's loving law obeys.
3 The early flowers bloom bright and fair,
  Fair shines the morning sky;

|:The birds make music in the air,:|
The brook goes singing by.
4 Like the spring morning, sweet and clear,
  That greets our gladdened eyes,
  |:The spring of heaven's eternal year:|
  Shall bring new earth and skies.

No. 77.   Come, ye Faithful.   Mozart.

1. Come, ye faith-ful, raise the strain Of tri-um-phant glad-ness,
God hath brought His earth a-gain, In-to joy from sad-ness,
Loosed from win-ter's i - cy yoke, Flow the leap-ing wa-ters;
Let your hearts flow forth in praise, All earth's sons and daugh-ters.

2 'Tis the Spring of souls to-day;
  Hope forever vernal,
  From the frost of fear and doubt,
  Springs in life eternal.
  All the winter of our griefs,
  Long and dark, be flying,
  In His light who gives to us
  Hope and faith undying.

3 Now the sower goeth forth,
  Seed of life to scatter,
  But the seed, to spring to life,
  Must its wrappings shatter.
  Ye, who bearing the precious seed,
  Go forth toiling, weeping,
  Know that He who with you works,
  Hath all in His keeping.

From "The Carol" by per. of The John Church Co.

No. 78. Come forth and Bring your Garlands.

To be sung in unison.
Moderato.
H. KOTZSCHMAR.

1. Come forth, and bring your gar-lands! Come forth with praise and song! Enwreath the al-tars with your flow'rs And to the tem-ples throng! For 'tis the glo-rious sum-mer, A time for glad-some praise, When all who love Earth's beau-ty May join our fes-tal lays.

2 Oh, what so sweet as summer,
   When all the sky is blue,
   And when the sunbeam's arrows
   Pierce all the green Earth through!
   And what so sweet as flowers,
   The blossoms white and red,
   Where troops of bright-wing'd insects
   Secure their daily bread!

3 Oh, what so sweet as birds are,
   That echo, in their trills,
   The music of the summer winds,
   The murmur of the rills!
   And all these sights and voices
   In garden, field and grove,
   Make Earth, array'd in beauty,
   A type of God's own love.

No. 79. The Spring-tide Hour.

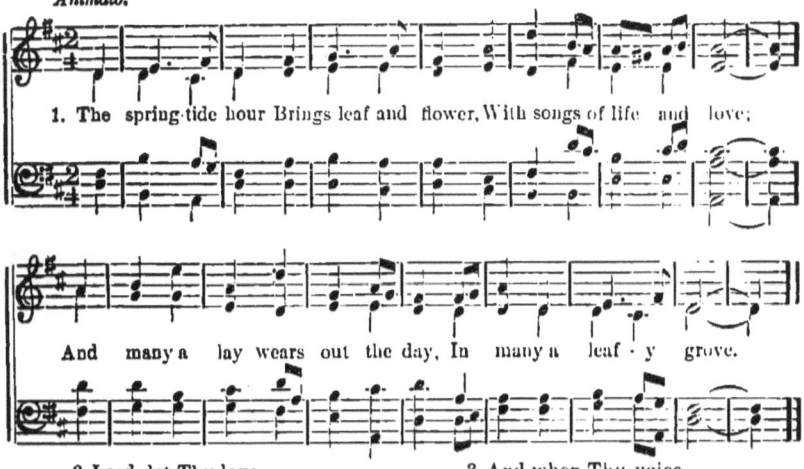

1. The spring-tide hour Brings leaf and flower, With songs of life and love; And many a lay wears out the day, In many a leaf-y grove.

2 Lord, let Thy love,
Fresh from above,
Soft as the south wind blow;
Call forth its bloom,
Wake its perfume,
And bid its spices flow.

3 And when Thy voice
Makes earth rejoice,
And the hills laugh and sing,
Lord, teach this heart
To bear its part,
And join the praise of spring.

No. 80. Days of Summer Glory.

GERMAN.

1. Days of sum-mer glo-ry, Days I love to see, All your scenes so bril-liant, They are dear to me.

2 Let our thoughts be ever
Pure as yonder sun:
Gentle as the breezes
When the night comes on.

3 Meadows, fields and mountains,
Clothed in shining green;
Little rippling fountains
Through the willows seen.

4 Birds that sweetly warble
All the summer days:
All things speak in music
Their Creator's praise.

No. 81. The Harvest Days.

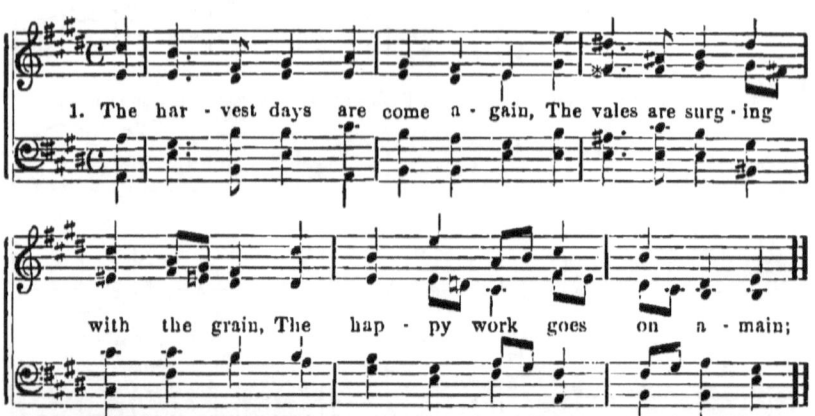

2 Pale streaks of cloud scarce veil the blue,
Against the golden harvest hue
The autumn trees look fresh and new;

3 And wrinkled brows relax with glee,
And aged eyes they laugh to see
The sickles follow o'er the lea.

4 The wains the sunny slopes roll down;
Afar the happy shout is blown
Of children, and of reapers brown.

5 May we into time's furrow cast
Our deeds, as seed-corn, thick and fast,
Whose fruit eternally shall last.

No. 82. Harvest Festival. CHARLES ZEUNER.

2 Lay all the bloom of gardens there,
And there the orchard fruits
Bring golden grain from sun and air,
From earth her goodly roots.

3 And let the common heart keep time
To such an anthem sung,

As never swelled on poet's rhyme
Or thrilled on singer's tongue.

4 A song of praise to Him who filled
The harvests far and near,
And gave each field a double yield
To crown the fruitful year.

From "The Gospel Hymner." of The John Church Co.

2 Thou only art the Maker
　Of all things near and far,
　The tint upon the rose leaf,
　The light within the star;
　The winds and waves obey Thee,
　The storms by Thee are led,
　On Thee all eyes are waiting,
　By Thee all creatures fed.

3 We thank Thee, O, our Father,
　For all things bright and good,
　The seed time and the harvest,
　Our life, our health, our food;
　Thine own kind hand hath kept us,
　Through all the changing year;
　Thy love it is that brings us,
　Again to worship here.

From "The Carol" by per. of The John Church C

No. 84. The Year is Swiftly Waning.

2 Oh! pour Thy grace upon us,
　That we may worthier be,
Each year that passes o'er us,
　To dwell in heaven with Thee.
Behold the bending orchards,
　With bounteous fruit are crowned;
Lord, in our hearts more richly,
　Let heavenly fruit abound.

3 Oh! by each mercy sent us,
　And by each grief and pain,
By blessings like the sunshine,
　And sorrow like the rain,
Our barren hearts make fruitful,
　With every goodly grace,
That in Thy name may hallow,
　And see at last Thy face.

No. 85. Winter's Blessing.
HAYDN.

1. "Tis win-ter now: The fall-en snow Has left the heavens all cold-ly clear; Thro' leaf-less boughs the sharp wind blows, And all the earth lies dead and drear.

2 And yet Thy love is not withdrawn;
  Thy life within the keen air breathes,
  Thy beauty paints the crimson dawn,
  And clothes the boughs with glitt'ring wreaths.
3 And tho' abroad the sharp wind blow,
  And skies are chill, and frosts are keen,

Home closer draws her circle now,
And warmer glows her light within.

4 O God, who giv'st the winter's cold,
  As well as summer's joyous rays,
  Still warmly in Thine arms enfold,
  And keep us thro' life's wintry days!

No. 86. God Shall Keep Thee.
SCHULTZ.

1. God shall charge His an-gel le-gions, Watch and ward o'er thee to keep,
2. Thou shalt call on Him in trou-ble, He will hearken, He will save;
Tho' thou walk thro' hos-tile re-gions, Tho' in des-ert wilds thou sleep.
Here for grief re-ward thee dou-ble, Crown with life be-yond the grave.

No. 87. Dedication Hymn.
(Italian Hymn.)

1. Praise ye the Lord, our King! Let all the nations sing, In one ac-cord. His glo-rious might and fame, His great and ho-ly name, Un-to the world proclaim— Praise ye the Lord!

2. E-ter-nal, High and great, To Thee we con-se-crate This sa-cred shrine. Our heart, our soul to Thee, We hal-low rev-'rent-ly, A sa-cred shrine to be, Sovereign di-vine!

3 What tongue is formed so well,
Of all Thy power to tell—
The fathomless.
Yet Thou art ever near,
Kindly to bend Thine ear,
Thy children's prayers to hear,
To hear and bless.

4 Here the glad truths reveal;
Here let the people kneel,
From nigh and far,
Blessing the Lord on high,
Maker of earth and sky,
Him, One in unity!
Hallelujah!

No. 88. God of all Nations.
(Tune No. 87 or America.)

1 God of the mighty hand,
Fount in the thirsty land,
Holy and pure:
All praise to Thee is due
By Israel's faithful few,
Who all Thy mercies know,
Thy covenant sure.

2 Thou, like a cloud of light,
Leading by day and night
Thy wandering fold,

Saved from oppression dire,
From wrathful sword and fire,
Thy praise our hearts inspire,
Now, as of old.

3 O God of truth and right,
Still lead us by Thy light,
Thy children all.
Soon may all nations know,
All sects and creeds below,
To Thee their praise they owe,
On Thee to call,

No. 89. America.

1. My coun-try! 'tis of thee, Sweet land of lib-er-ty,
2. My na-tive coun-try, thee, Land of the no-ble free,

Of thee I sing: Land where my fa-thers died! Land of the
Thy name I love; I love thy rocks and rills, Thy woods and

pil-grim's pride! From ev-'ry moun-tain side Let free-dom ring!
tem-pled hills: My heart with rapt-ure thrills Like that a-bove.

3 Let music swell the breeze,
And ring from all the trees
Sweet freedom's song:
Let mortal tongues awake;
Let all that breathe partake;
Let rocks their silence break,
The sound prolong.

4 Our fathers' God, to Thee,
Author of liberty,
To Thee we sing:
Long may our land be bright
With freedom's holy light;
Protect us by Thy might,
Great God, our King!

No. 90. Our Native Land.

1 God bless our native land!
Firm may she ever stand,
Through storm and night:
When the wild tempests rave,
Ruler of wind and wave,
Do Thou our country save
By Thy great might!

2 For her our prayer shall rise
To God above the skies;
On Him we wait:
Thou who art ever nigh,
Guarding with watchful eye,
To Thee aloud we cry,
God save the State!

No. 91. Our Soldiers' Graves.

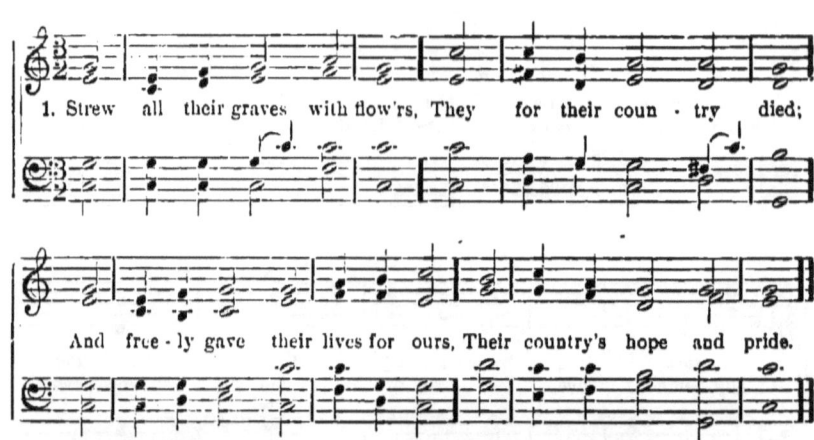

1. Strew all their graves with flow'rs, They for their coun-try died;
And free-ly gave their lives for ours, Their country's hope and pride.

2 Bring flowers to deck each sod,
　Where rests their sacred dust;
Though gone from earth, they live to God,
　Their everlasting trust!

3 Fearless, in freedom's cause,
　They suffered, toiled and bled;
And died, obedient to her laws,
　By truth and conscience led.

4 Oft as the year returns,
　She o'er their graves shall weep,
And wreath with flowers their funeral urns
　Their memory dear to keep.

5 Bring flowers of early spring
　To deck each soldier's grave:
And summer's fragrant roses bring—
　They died our land to save.

From "The Carol" by per. of The John Church Co.

No. 92. Our Country.

J. H. KNECHT.

1. O beau-ti-ful, my coun-try! Be thine a no-bler care,
Than all thy wealth of com-merce, Thy har-vest wav-ing fair,

Our Country. Concluded.

2 For thee ourfathers suffered,
  For thee they toiled and prayed;
  Upon thy holy altar
  Their willing lives they laid.
  Thou hast no common birthright;
  Grand memories on thee shine,
  The blood of pilgrim nations
  Commingled, flows in thine.

3 O beautiful, our country!
  Round thee in love we draw,
  Thine is the grace of freedom,
  The majesty of law.
  Be righteousness thy sceptre,
  Justice thy diadem;
  And on thy shining forehead
  Be peace the crowning gem.

No. 93.   God's Abode.

H G NÆGELI.

2 Where'er ascends the sacrifice
  Of fervent praise and prayer,
  Or on the earth, or in the skies,
  The heaven of God is there.

3 His presence there is spread abroad
  Thro' realms, thro' worlds unknown;
  Who seeks the mercies of His God
  Is ever near His throne.

No. 94. Flag of the Free.

HARRISON MILLARD.

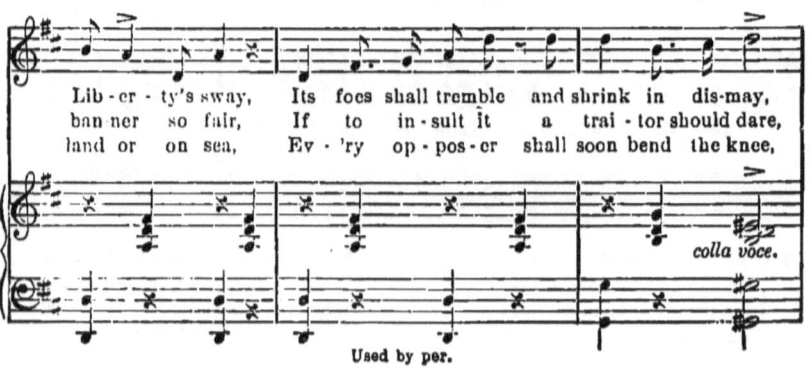

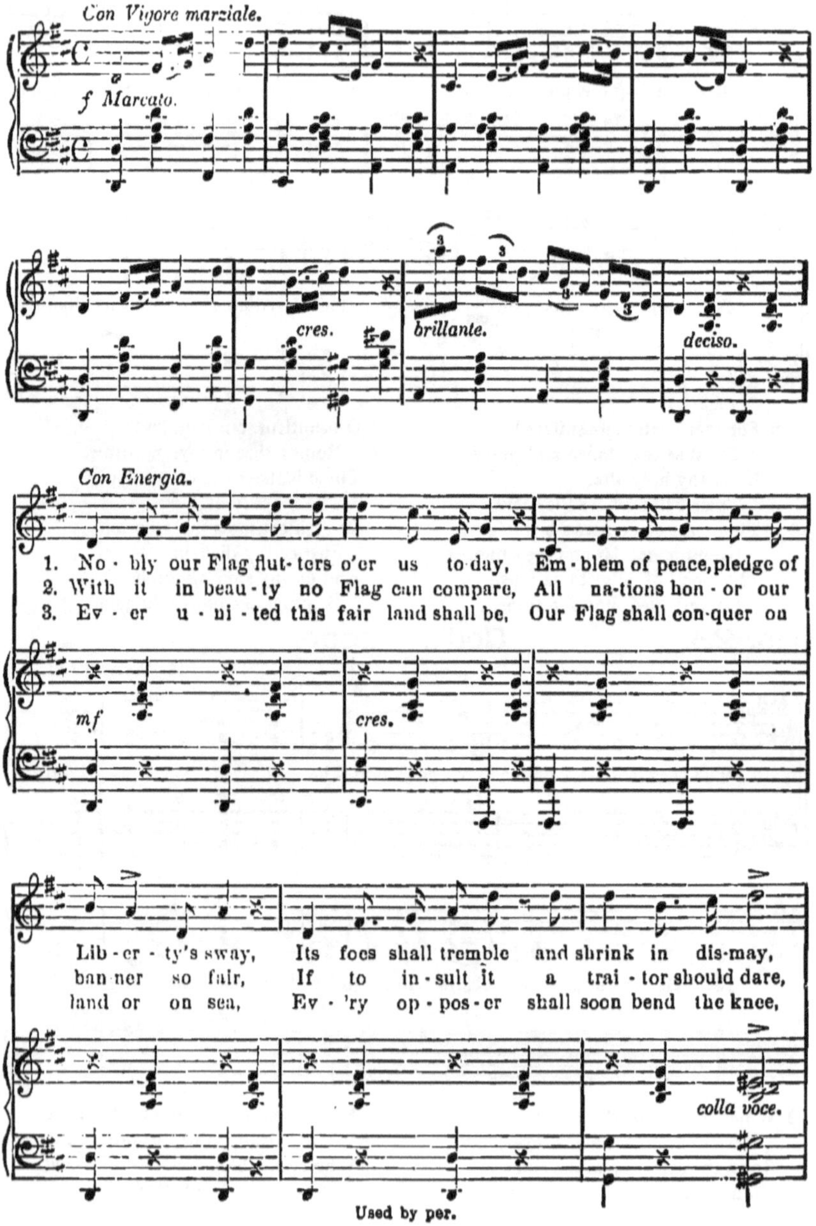
Con Vigore marziale.
f Marcato.
cres.
brillante.
deciso.
Con Energia.
1. No - bly our Flag flut - ters o'er us to - day, Em - blem of peace, pledge of
2. With it in beau - ty no Flag can compare, All na-tions hon - or our
3. Ev - er u - ni - ted this fair land shall be, Our Flag shall con - quer on
mf
cres.
Lib - er - ty's sway, Its foes shall tremble and shrink in dis - may,
ban - ner so fair, If to in - sult it a trai - tor should dare,
land or on sea, Ev - 'ry op - pos - er shall soon bend the knee,
colla voce.

Used by per.

Flag of the Free. Concluded.

No. 95. God Ever Glorious.

With sustained tone.

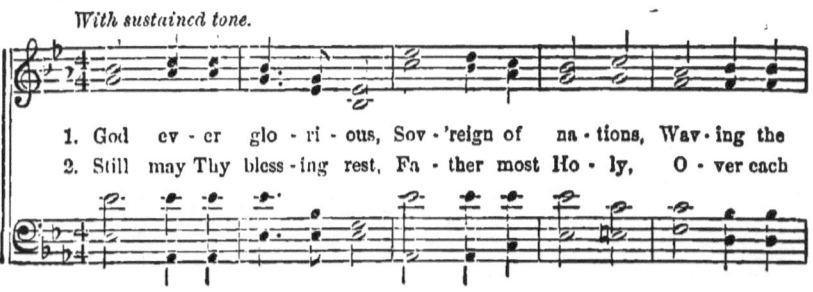

1. God ev-er glo-ri-ous, Sov-'reign of na-tions, Wav-ing the
2. Still may Thy bless-ing rest, Fa-ther most Ho-ly, O-ver each

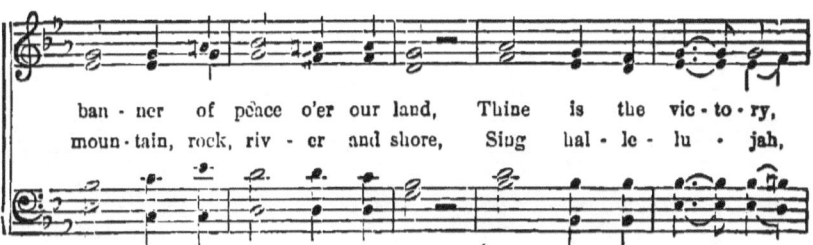

ban-ner of peace o'er our land, Thine is the vic-to-ry,
moun-tain, rock, riv-er and shore, Sing hal-le-lu-jah,

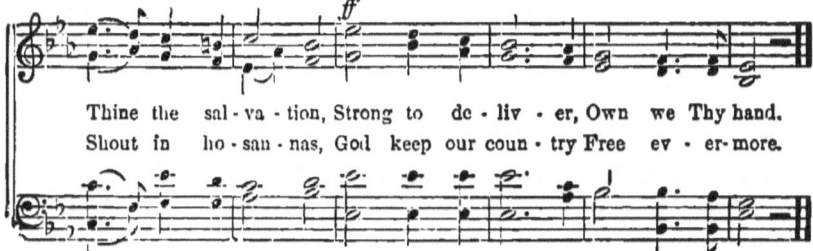

Thine the sal-va-tion, Strong to de-liv-er, Own we Thy hand.
Shout in ho-san-nas, God keep our coun-try Free ev-er-more.

No. 96. Fatherland.

Tune: America.

1 To thee, O Fatherland,
Bon i of our heart and hand,
Rolls our high song.
May all thy path-ways be
Highways of Liberty,
And Justice, throned in thee,
Reign ages long!

2 And Thou, O God of Right,
The Lord, whose arm of might,
Our Fathers bore,—
Thou mad'st their children strong
To break the chains of wrong,
Till rang the Freeman's song
From shore to shore.

3 Free as our rivers flow,
Pure as our breezes blow,
Be our broad land!
Bright home of Liberty,
High hope of all the free—
Our love thy watch-tower be,
Dear Fatherland!

No. 97. The Star-Spangled Banner.

SOLO.   FRANCIS S. KEY.

1. O say, can you see by the dawn's ear-ly light,
Whose broad stripes and bright stars, through the per-il-ous fight,

2. On the shore dim-ly seen, through the mists of the deep,
What is that which the breeze o'er the tow-er-ing steep,

What so proud-ly we hailed at the twi-light's last gleam-ing,
O'er the ram-parts we watched, were so gal-lant-ly stream-ing?

Where the foe's haughty host in dread si-lence re-pos-es,
As it fit-ful-ly blows, half con-ceals, half dis-clos-es?

And the rock-et's red glare, the bombs bursting in air, Gave
Now it catch-es the gleam of the morn-ing's first beam, In full

proof thro' the night, that our flag was still there. O say, does the star-spangled
glo-ry re-flect-ed, now shines on the stream: 'Tis the star-spangled banner, O

ban-ner yet wave, O'er the land of the free and the home of the brave?
long may it wave O'er the land of the free and the home of the brave!

The Star-Spangled Banner. Concluded.

3 And where is the band who so vauntingly swore,
That the havoc of war and the battle's confusion,
A home and a country they'd leave us no more?
Their blood has washed out their foul footsteps' pollution;
No refuge could save the hireling and slave
From the terror of flight or the gloom of the grave,
And the star-spangled banner in triumph shall wave
O'er the land of the free and the home of the brave!

4 Oh! thus be it ever when freemen shall stand
Between their lov'd home and the war's desolation;
Blest with vict'ry and peace, may the heav'n-rescued land
Praise the Power that hath made and preserv'd us a nation.
Then conquer we must, when our cause it is just,
And this be our motto, "In God is our trust,"
And the star-spangled banner in triumph shall wave
O'er the land of the free and the home of the brave!

No. 98. Land of Our Fathers.

Moderato. S. WEBBE. (1740-1816.)

1. Land of our fa-thers! where-so-e'er we roam; Land of our birth; to u thou still art home; Peace and pros-per-i-ty on thy sons at-tend; Down to pos-ter-i-ty their in-flu-ence de-scends;
2. Tho' oth-er climes may bright-er hopes ful-fill, Land of our birth! we ev-er love thee still; Heav'n shield our happy home from each hostile band; Free-dom and plen-ty ev-er crown our na-tive land;

D. C.—All then in-vit-ing, hearts and voic-es join-ing, Sing we in har-mo-ny our na-tive land.

O Rest in the Lord. Continued.

O Rest in the Lord. Concluded.

No. 101. **The Eternal Goodness.**

RICHARD STORRS WILLIS.

1. I see the wrong that round me lies, I feel the guilt with-in,
2. I dim-ly guess from blessings known, Of great-er out of sight,
3. And so be-side the si-lent sea, I wait with muf-fled oar;

I hear with groan and trav-ail cries The world con-fess its sin.
And with the chastened psalm-ist own His judgments, too, are right.
No harm can come from Him to me, On o-cean or on shore.

Yet in the maddening maze of things, And tossed by storm and flood,
I know not what the fu-ture hath Of mar-vel or sur-prise,
I know not where His isl-ands lift Their frond ed palms in air;

To one fixed stake my spir-it clings: I know that God is good.
As-sured a-lone that life and death His mer-cy un-der-lies.
I on-ly know I can-not drift Be-yond His love and care.

No. 102. Who Is Like Thee?

Arr. by WM. OTIS BREWSTER.

1. Who is like Thee, O U-ni-ver-sal Lord! Who dare Thy praise and glory share? Who is in heav'n, Most High, like Thee a-dored? Who can on earth with Thee compare? Thou art the one true God a-lone, And firm-ly found-ed is Thy throne.

2 Thy tender love embraces all mankind,　　Thy hand upholdeth the opprest;
　As children all by Thee are blest;　　　　All worlds attest Thy power sublime,
　Repentant sinners with Thee mercy find,　 Thy glory shines in every clime.

No. 103. The Heavens Declare.

(*Tune 30*)

1 The heavens declare Thy glory, Lord,
　Which that alone can fill;
　The firmament and stars express
　Their great Creator's skill.

2 The dawn of each returning day
　Fresh beams of knowledge brings;
　And from the dark returns of night
　Divine instruction springs.

3 Their powerful language to no realm
　Or region is confined;
　'Tis nature's voice, and understood
　Alike by all mankind.

4 The statutes of the Lord are just,
　And bring sincere delight;
　His pure commands, in search of truth,
　Assist the feeblest sight.

Songs of Duty.

No. 104. The Call to Duty.

1. All around us, fair with flowers, Fields of beauty sleeping lie;
All around us, clarion voices Call to duty, stern and high.

2 Following every voice of mercy,
With a trusting, loving heart,
Let us in life's earnest labor
Still be sure to do our part.

3 Now, to-day, and not to-morrow,
Let us work with all our might,

Lest the wretched faint and perish
In the coming stormy night.

4 Now, to-day, and not to-morrow,
Lest before to-morrow's sun,
We too, mournfully departing,
Shall have left our work undone.

No. 105. The Law Within.

1. Say not the law divine...... Is hidden from thee, or afar removed; That law within would
2. Soar not on high,...... Nor ask who thence shall bring it down to earth. That vaulted

The Law Within. Concluded.

shine,   If there its   glo - rious light were sought and loved.
sky.... Hath no such star, did'st thou but know its worth.

3 Nor launch thy bark
In search thereof, upon a shoreless sea,
Which has no ark,   [thee.
No dove to bring this olive branch to

4 Then do not roam   [not win:
In search of that which wandering can
At home! at home!   [within.
There peace is found, thy very heart

No. 106.   Be True.

1. 'Be true to ev - 'ry in - most thought; Be as thy
thought, thy speech;...... What thou hast not by
suf - f'ring bought, Pre - sume not thou to teach......

2 Woe, woe to him on safety bent,
   Who creeps to age from youth,
   Failing to grasp his life's intent,
   Because he fears the truth.

3 Show forth thy light! If conscience
   Cherish the rising glow,   [gleam,
   The smallest spark may shed its beam,
   O'er thousand hearts below.

4 Guard thou the fact! Tho' clouds of night
   Down on thy watch-tower stoop;
   Tho' thou should'st see thy heart's delight
   Borne from thee by their swoop,

5 Face thou the wind! Tho' safer seem
   In shelter to abide;
   We were not made to sit and dream;
   The true must first be tried.

No. 107. One By One

1. One by one the sands are flowing, One by one the moments fall,
Some are com-ing, Some are go-ing, Do not strive to grasp them all.

2 One by one thy duties wait thee,
  Let thy whole strength go to each;
  Let no future dreams elate thee,
  Learn thou first what these can teach;

3 One by one thy griefs shall meet thee,
  Do not fear an arméd band;
  One will fade as others greet thee,
  Shadows passing thro' the land.

4 Do not linger with regretting
  Or for passing hours despond;
  Nor, the daily toil forgetting,
  Look too eagerly beyond.

5 Every hour that fleets so slowly,
  Has its task to do or bear;
  Luminous the crown, and holy,
  When each gem is set with care.

No. 108. Live for Something.

1. Live for something; Be not I-dle, Look a-bout thee for em-ploy;
Sit not down to use-less dreaming, La-bor is the sweet-est joy.
Fold-ed hands are ev-er wea-ry, Selfish hearts are nev-er gay;

Live for Something. Concluded.

As the pleasant sunshine falleth,
Ever on the grateful earth,
So, let sympathy and kindness
‖:Gladden well the darken'd hearth.:‖

3 Hearts that are oppressed and weary,
Drop the tear of sympathy;
Whisper words of hope and comfort,
Give, and thy reward shall be
Joy unto thy soul returning,
From this perfect fountain-head;
Freely, as thou freely givest,
‖:Shall the grateful light be shed,:‖

2 Scatter blessings in your pathway,—
Gentle words and cheering smiles;
Better far than gold and silver
Are their grief-dispelling wiles

No. 109.   The Builders.

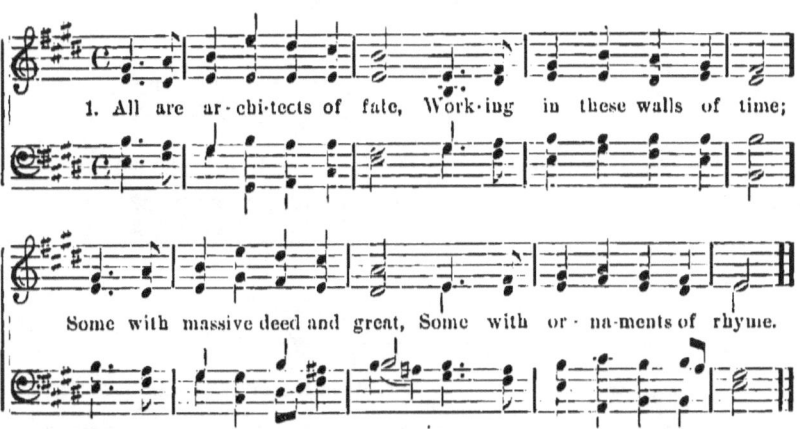

2 Nothing useless is, or low,
  Each thing in its place is best;
  And what seems but idle show
  Strengthens and supports the rest.

3 For the structure that we raise,
  Time is with materials filled;

Our to-days and yester-days
Are the blocks with which we build

5 Build to-day, then, strong and sure,
  With a firm and ample base;
  And ascending and secure,
  Shall to-morrow find its place.

No. 110.   Happiness.

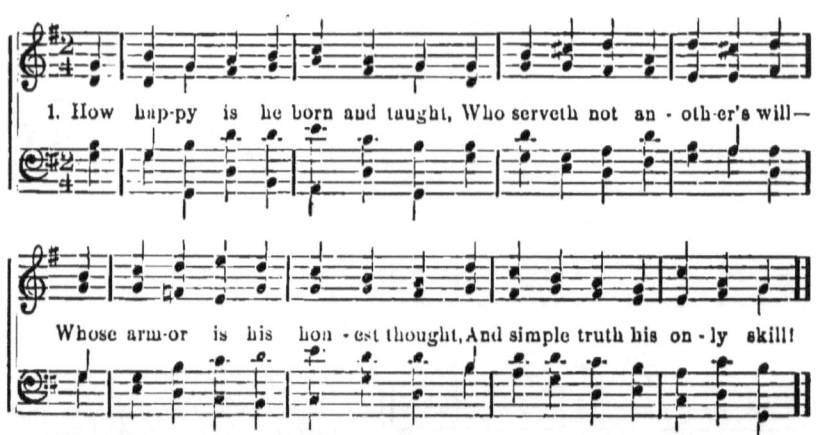

2 Whose passions not his masters are,
  Whose soul is still prepared for death,
  Untied to this vain world by care
  Of public fame or private breath!

3 This man is freed from servile bands,
  Of hope to rise, or fear to fall;
  Lord of himself, though not of lands,
  And having nothing, yet hath all.

No. 111.   The Wealth of the Heart.

From SCHUMANN.

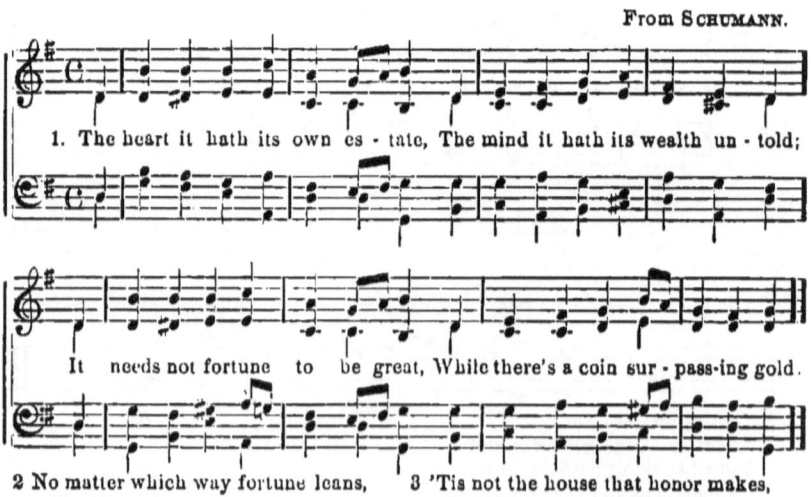

2 No matter which way fortune leans,
  Wealth makes not happiness secure;
  A little mind hath little means,
  A narrow heart is always poor.

3 'Tis not the house that honor makes,
  True honor is a thing divine;
  It is the mind precedence takes,
  It is the spirit makes the shrine.

No. 112   The Voice of Conscience.

S. W. WILKINSON.

1. There lives a voice with-in me, Guest-an-gel of my heart,
   world is full of beau-ty, The cold-est heart to move,

Whose whisp'rings strive to win me To act the man-ful part.
And if we did our du-ty, It might be full of love.

Up ev-er more it spring-eth Like some sweet mel-o-dy,

And ev-er-more it sing-eth This sa-cred truth to me: This

2 The leaf-tongue of the forest
   The flower-lips of the sod;
   The birds that hymn their raptures
   Up to the throne of God,
   The summer wind that bringeth
   Joy over land and sea,
   Have each a voice that singeth
   This blessed truth to me:
   This world is full of beauty, etc.

3 Oh, voice of God most tender
   Oh, voice of God divine,
   Still be my heart's defender
   Till every thought is Thine.
   My soul in gladness bringeth
   Its song of praise to Thee,
   While all around me singeth
   This holy truth to me:
   This world is full of beauty, etc.

From "The Carol" by per. of The John Church Co.

No. 113. Do Thy Duty!

2 Faint not! yield not! 'tis no sadness
Burdens thee on life's true way:
Duty done is heart-felt gladness,
Cheering as the summer ray:
Do thy duty, tide what may!

3 When a cloud obscures the heaven,
Know the sun will bring thee day:
When to grief thy soul is given,
Trust that love will ever stay.
Do thy duty, tide what may!

4 All the trials that surround thee
Are but stones to mark thy way:
Nought will baffle or confound thee,
Canst thou love, and bravely say:
Do thy duty, tide what may!

No. 114. Life Is Onward!

Life Is Onward! Concluded.

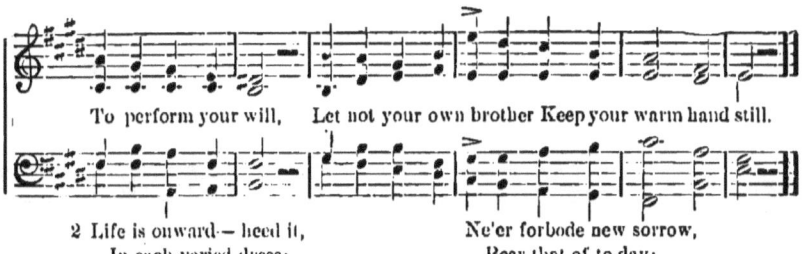

To perform your will, Let not your own brother Keep your warm hand still.

2 Life is onward— heed it,
In each varied dress;
Your own act can speed it
On to happiness.
His bright pinion o'er you,
Time waves not in vain,
If hope chants before you
Her prophetic strain.

3 Life is onward— never
Look upon the past,
It would hold you ever
In its fetters fast.

Ne'er forbode new sorrow,
Bear that of to-day;
Thou shalt see the morrow
Chase the clouds away.

4 Life is onward—treasure
Its eternal part,
Give it without measure
All thy strength of heart.
Life is onward— prize it,
Sunlit or in storm;
Oh do not despise it
In its humblest form!

No. 115. The Law of Love.

1. Pour forth the oil,—pour bold - ly forth: It will not fail, un - til....
Thou fail - est ves - sels to pro - vide, Which it may large - ly fill.......

2 Make channels for the streams of love,
Where they may broadly run;
And love has overflowing streams,
To fill them every one.

3 But if at any time we cease
Such channels to provide,

The very founts of love for us
Will soon be parched and dried.

4 For we must share, if we would keep
That blessing from above;
Ceasing to give, we cease to have,
Such is the law of love.

No. 117. There's Work to Do.

With energy.

1. Rouse up to work that waits for us, O spend-thrifts of to-day!
We'll make our dai-ly rec-ord A grand one while we may.

REFRAIN.
There's work to do, there's work to do, To help our fel-low-man.
In earth's great field of la-bor, We'll do the best we can.

2 Shake off the sloth that fetters us,
  Put on the will that wins:
The battle, for the earnest,
  In their own heart begins.

3 No nobler hero in the fight,
  Since battle-fields began,

Than he who serves the right,
  And does the best he can.

4 So work while day is passing;
  And at life's setting sun,
When all our sheaves are gathered,
  Shall truest peace be won.

No. 118. Who Is Thy Neighbor?

2 Thy neighbor? 'Tis the fainting poor,
  Whose eye with want is dim:
  Oh, enter thou his humble door,
  With aid and peace for him.

3 Thy neighbor? He who drinks the cup,
  When sorrow drowns the brim;
  With words of high, sustaining hope,
  Go thou and comfort him.

4 Thy neighbor? 'Tis the weary slave,
  Fettered in mind and limb;
  He hath no hope this side the grave
  Go thou, and ransom him.

5 Thy neighbor? Pass no mourner by;
  Perhaps thou canst redeem
  A breaking heart from misery;
  Go share thy lot with him.

No. 119. How Skillful grows the Hand.

How Skillful grows the Hand. Concluded.

to the high-est doth at-tain, To the high-est doth at-tain.
That o-bey-eth love's com-mand, That o-bey-eth love's command.

No. 120. The Future.

1. The fu-ture hides in it Gladness and sorrow;
We press still tho-row, Naught that a-bides in it

Daunt-ing us,— on-ward!

2 And solemn before us,
Veiled the dark portal;
Goal of all mortal:—
Stars silent o'er us,
Graves under us silent.

3 While earnest thou gazest,
Comes boding of terror,
Come phantasm and error;
Perplexing the bravest
With doubt and misgiving.

4 But heard are the voices,
Heard are the sages,
The worlds, and the ages:
"Choose well; your choice is
Brief, and yet endless."

5 "Here eyes do regard you,
In eternity's stillness;
Here is all fulness,
Ye brave, to reward you;
Work, and despair not!"

No. 121. Moral Influence.

1. When-e'er a no-ble deed is wrought, When-e'er is spok'n a no-ble thought, Our hearts, in glad sur-prise, To high-er lev-els rise ....

2 The tidal wave of deeper souls
Into our inmost being rolls,
And lifts us unawares
Out of all deeper cares.

3 Honor to those whose words and deeds
Thus help us in our daily needs,
And by their overflow
Raise us from what is low.

No. 122. Charity.

From SPOHR.

1. Hon-or to him who free-ly gives Of his a-bun-dant store;........ Who shares the gifts that he re-ceives With those who need them more; Whose melt-ing heart of

Charity. Concluded.

2 Honor to him who shuns to do
  An action mean or low;
  Who will a nobler course pursue
  To stranger, friend or foe;
  Who seeks for justice more than gain,
  Is merciful and kind;
  Who will not cause a needless pain
  In body or in mind.

3 Honor to him who scorns to be
  To name or sect a slave;
  Whose soul is like the sunshine, free,
  Free as the ocean wave;
  Who, when he sees oppression, wrong,
  Speaks out in thunder-tones;
  Who feels that he with truth is strong,
  To grapple e'en with thrones.

No. 123. Gentleness.

2 Speak gently to the young, for they
  Will have enough to bear;
  Pass through this life as best they may,
  'Tis full of anxious care.

3 Speak gently to the aged one,
  Grieve not the care-worn heart;
  The sands of life are nearly run,
  Let them in peace depart,

4 Speak gently to the erring ones,
  They must have toiled in vain;
  Perchance unkindness made them so;
  Oh! win them back again.

5 Speak gently! —'tis a little thing
  Dropp'd in the heart's deep well;
  The good, the joy, that it may bring
  Eternity shall tell.

The Golden City. Concluded.

ban-ished from its bor-ders, Jus-tice reigns su-preme o'er all

2. We are builders of that city,
   All our joys and all our groans
   Help to rear its shining ramparts,
   All our lives are building-stones:
   But the work that we have builded,
   Oft with bleeding hands and tears,
   And in error and in anguish,
   Will not perish with the years,
   But the work that we have builded
   Will not perish with the years.

3. It will be, at last made perfect,
   In the universal plan,
   It will help to crown the labors
   Of the toiling hosts of man;
   It will last and shine transfigured
   In the final reign of right.
   It will merge into the splendors
   Of the City of the Light.
   It will merge into the splendors
   Of the City of the Light.

No. 125. Say Not They Die.

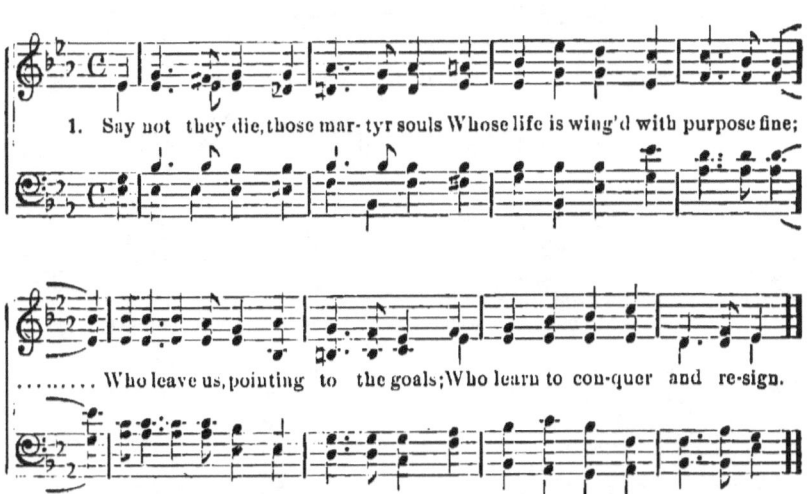

1. Say not they die, those mar-tyr souls Whose life is wing'd with purpose fine;
   .... Who leave us, pointing to the goals; Who learn to con-quer and re-sign.

2. Such cannot die; they vanquish time,
   And fill the world with growing light,
   Making the human life sublime
   With memories of their sacred might.

3. They cannot die whose lives are part
   Of that great life which is to be,
   Whose hearts beat with the world's great heart,
   And throb with its high destiny.

4. Then mourn not those who, dying, gave
   A gift of greater light to man:
   Death stands abashed before the brave;
   They own a life he may not ban.

Let in Light. Concluded.

2 I will hope and work and love,
Singing to the hours,
While the stars are bright above,
And below the flowers.

Who in such a world as this
Could not heal his sorrow?
Welcome this sweet hour of bliss;
Sunrise comes tomorrow.

No. 127. The Gain of Man.

2 That all of good the past hath had,
Remains to make our own time glad;
Our common daily life divine,
And every land a Palestine.

3 For still the new transcends the old
In signs and tokens manifold;
Slaves rise up men, the olive waves
With roots deep set in battle graves.

4 Through the harsh noises of our day,
A low sweet prelude finds its way:
Thro' clouds of doubt and creeds of fear
A light is breaking, calm and clear.

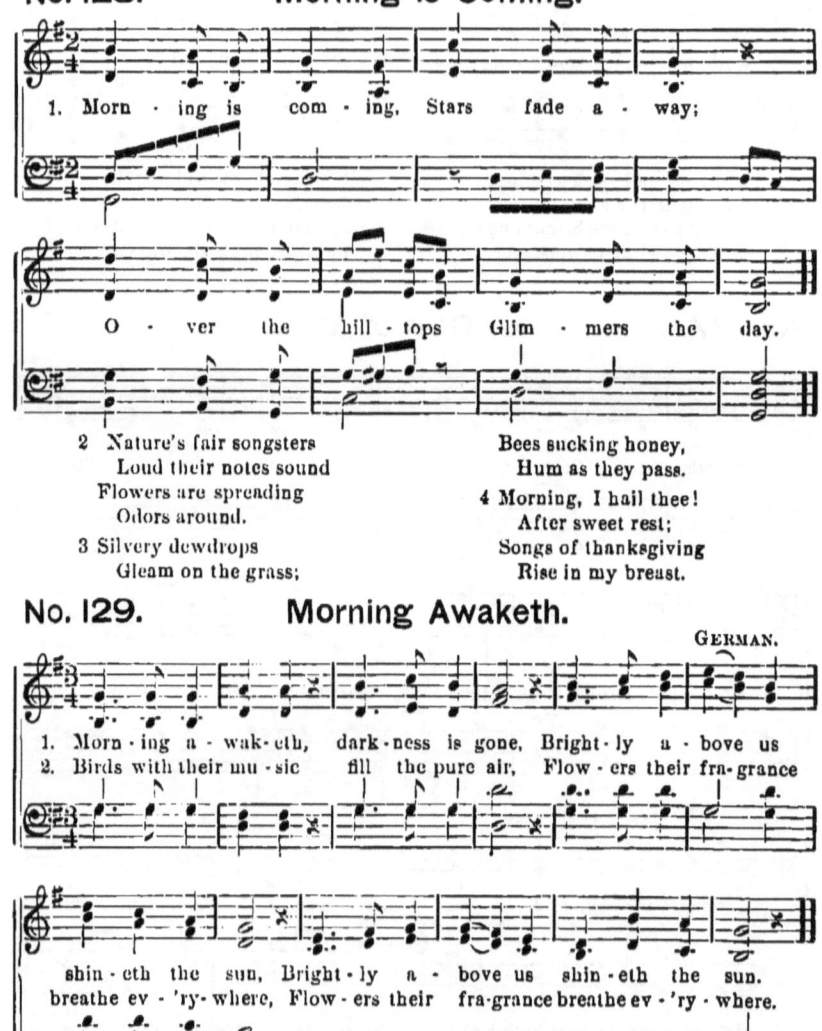

Songs for the Primary Classes.

No. 128.   Morning is Coming.

1. Morn-ing is com-ing, Stars fade a-way;
O-ver the hill-tops Glim-mers the day.

2 Nature's fair songsters
  Loud their notes sound
  Flowers are spreading
  Odors around.

3 Silvery dewdrops
  Gleam on the grass;

  Bees sucking honey,
  Hum as they pass.

4 Morning, I hail thee!
  After sweet rest;
  Songs of thanksgiving
  Rise in my breast.

No. 129.   Morning Awaketh.

GERMAN.

1. Morn-ing a-wak-eth, dark-ness is gone, Bright-ly a-bove us shin-eth the sun, Bright-ly a-bove us shin-eth the sun.
2. Birds with their mu-sic fill the pure air, Flow-ers their fra-grance breathe ev-'ry-where, Flow-ers their fra-grance breathe ev-'ry-where.

3 Brightly the dew drops spangle the grass;   4 All is so joyful, all is so blest,
  Bees in the meadows hum as they pass.   Praises and joy should fill every breast.

130. Who Taught the Bird?

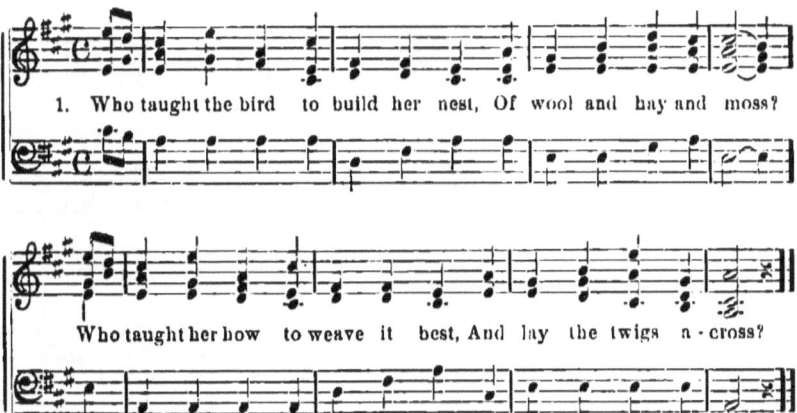

1. Who taught the bird to build her nest, Of wool and hay and moss?
Who taught her how to weave it best, And lay the twigs a-cross?

2 Who taught the busy bee to fly
Among the sweetest flowers.
And lay her store of honey by
To last in winter's hours?

3 Who taught the little ant the way
Its narrow hole to bore,
And thro' the pleasant summer day,
To gather up its store?

4 'Twas God who taught them all the way,
And gave their little skill;
He teaches children when they pray
To do His holy will

No. 131. Little Drops of Water.

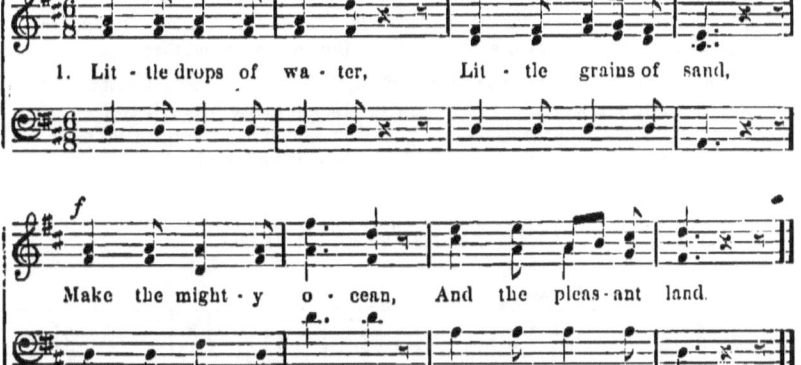

1. Lit-tle drops of wa-ter, Lit-tle grains of sand,
Make the might-y o-cean, And the pleas-ant land.

2 And the little moments,
Humble though they be,
Make the mighty ages
Of eternity.

3 Little deeds of kindness,
Little words of love,
Make our earth an Eden,
Like the heaven above.

No. 132. I Sing the Almighty Power of God.

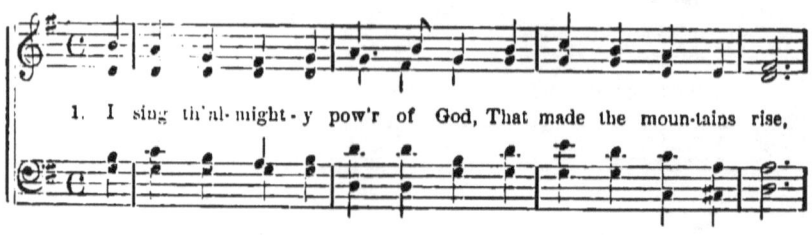

2 I sing the wisdom that ordained
   The sun to rule the day,
The moon shines full at His command,
   And all the stars obey.

3 I sing the goodness of the Lord,
   That filled the earth with food,
He formed the creatures with His word,
   And then pronounced them good.

4 Lord, how Thy wonders are displayed,
   Where'er I turn my eye,
If I survey the ground I tread,
   Or gaze upon the sky.

5 Ther's not a plant or flow'r below,
   But makes Thy glories known,
And clouds arise, and tempests blow,
   By order from Thy throne.

6 Creatures, as numerous as they be,
   Are subject to Thy care,
There's not a place where we can flee,
   But God is present there.

7 His hand is my perpetual guard,
   He guides me with His eye,
How should I then forget the Lord,
   Who is forever nigh?

No. 133.   The Stars Watch You.

The Stars Watch You. Concluded.

2 All you do and all you say,
   He can see and hear;
   When you work and when you play,
   Think the Lord is near,
   Think the Lord is near!

3 All your joys and griefs He knows
   Counts each falling tear;
   When to Him you tell your woes,
   Think the Lord will hear,
   Think the Lord will hear!

4 What we do as in His sight,
   We can do with ease;
   Every task becomes more light,
   When we think He sees,
   When we think He sees.

No. 134. None Is Like God.

2 In all the earth there is no spot
   Excluded from His care,
   We cannot go where God is not,
   For He is everywhere.

3 He sees us when we are alone,
   Though no one else can see,
   And all our thoughts to Him are known,
   Wherever we may be.

4 He is our best and kindest friend,
   And guards us night and day,
   To all our wants He will attend,
   And answer when we pray.

5 Oh! if we love Him as we ought,
   And on His grace rely,
   We shall be joyful at the thought
   That God is always nigh.

NO. 135. Brightly glows the Day.

1. Bright-ly glows the day, Night has fled a-way.

Ev-'ry joy-ful sound E-choes all a-round.

2 Sweet is morn to me,
Thanks, O God, to Thee!
Thou a guard hast kept,
O'er me while I slept.

3 Hear me while I raise
This my song of praise;
May my heart each day,
To Thee ever pray.

No. 136. God Made the Sun.

1. God made the sun, that world of light; The moon to cheer the earth by night; The clouds that float in

God Made the Sun. Concluded.

air so high, And all the stars that gild the sky.

2 He made the earth on which we tread,
And round its shores the ocean spread;
He made the seasons of the year,
And all the numerous fruits they bear.

3 He made the birds that sing so sweet,
The little lambs that frisk and bleat;

The playful fishes in the stream,
And beasts of every size and name.

4 It is by His kind grace and care,
We see, and feel, and speak and hear;
Our hands, our head, our heart, he gave,
And made our soul, we hope, to save.

No. 137. God Make My Life.

1. God make my life a lit-tle light, With-in the world to glow;

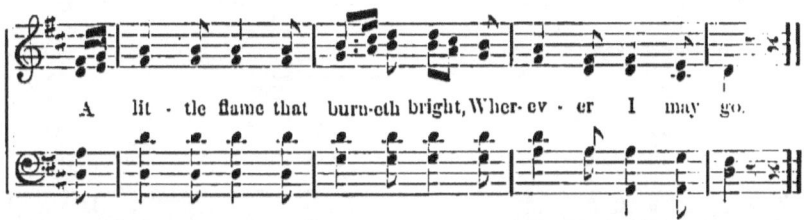

A lit-tle flame that burn-eth bright, Wher-ev-er I may go.

2 God make my life a little flower,
That giveth joy to all,
Content to bloom in native bower,
Although its place be small.

3 God make my life a little song,
That comforteth the sad;

That helpeth others to be strong,
And makes the singer glad.

4 God make my life a little hymn
Of tenderness and praise;
Of faith that never waxeth dim,
In all His wondrous ways.

From "Good Words."

No. 138. God Is Always Near Me.

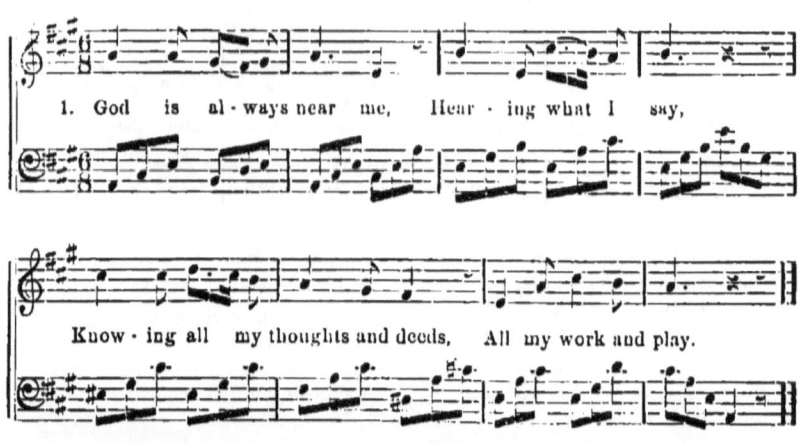

1. God is al-ways near me, Hear-ing what I say,
Know-ing all my thoughts and deeds, All my work and play.

2 God is always near me,
In the darkest night
He can see me just the same
As by mid-day light.

3 God is always near me,
Though so young and small,
Not a look, or word, or thought,
But God knows it all.

No. 139. See the Rain is Falling.

1. See the rain is fall-ing, On the moun-tain's side!

See the clouds dis-pers-ing, Bless-ings far and wide.

2 See the cooling shower
Comes at God's command,
Brightens every flower,
Cheers the parched land.

3 When the rain is over,
Then the painted bow

O'er the cloudy hill-top
Will its colors show.

4 God is ever faithful,
God is ever true;
Let us all be grateful
For the rain and dew.

No. 140. The Voice Within.

1. The still small voice that speaks with-in, I hear it, when at play, I speak the loud and an-gry word, That drives my friend a-way.

CHORUS.
The voice with-in, the voice with-in, Oh, may I have a care; It speaks to warn from ev-'ry sin, And God has placed it there.

2 If falsehood whispers to my heart
　To tell a coward lie,
To hide some careless thing I've done,
　I hear the sad voice nigh.

3 If selfishness would bid me keep
　What I should gladly share,
I hear again the inner voice,
　And then with shame forbear

4 I thank thee, Father, for this friend,
　Whom I would always heed;
Oh, may I hear the slightest tone
　In every time of need.

From "The Carol" by per. of The John Church Co., owners of copyright.

No. 141. The Sunny Side.

1. A sil-v'ry tide, called "Sun-ny Side", Goes creep-ing round the earth, And nev-er a place, but wins a grace, In the ju-bi-lant flood of mirth; From the danc-ing gleam on the fret-ted stream, To the dim-ple on ba-by's cheek, That in and out to his mer-ry shout Twink-les a hide-and-seek.

2 Wherever it goes the darkness glows,
And men and women sing;
It fills their eyes with a glad surprise
And stays their sorrowing.
The heart is a tune, the world is June,
Nothing is old or gray,
As it passes along with the swell of a song
Like the musical break of day.

3 Spirit of Love, in the blue above
Who makest the sun to flame,
Who guidest the flight of the planets bright,
And callest the stars by name.
It is Thou dost hide in the "Sunny Side"
And movest from heart to heart!
And, soul or clod, we are of the God
Who comes,—and the shadows part.

No. 142. The Spring Flowers.

1. The Spring has called us from our sleep, And from the

ground we glad-ly peep; We love to hear her gen-tle

call, And come to greet her, one and all.

2 I am a tiny daisy bright,
   With golden eye and petals white,
   Among the grass I have my place,
   And starlike is my little face.

3 My stalk is green and very tall,
   At night I am a yellow ball;
   But in the morning when I wake,
   A lovely little cup I make.

4 I am the blue forget-me-not,
   The banks of streams my fav'rite spot;
   I am the color of the sky,
   Except my round and sunny eye.

5 A thorny bramble bush am I,
   Swinging my flow'ry branches high;
   But fruit will come, O, what a treat,
   For all of you to pick and eat.

6 I am the sweet, perfumèd rose,
   The queen of every flower that grows;
   My blossoms show that Spring is past,
   And the bright Summer come at last.

7 We children thus the Spring may greet
   With joy in all its blessings sweet;
   For children's little lives appear
   Like the first blossoms of the year.

No. 143. The Rose Is Queen.

Tune 36.

1 The rose is queen among the flowers,
　None other is so fair;
　The lily nodding on her stem,
　With fragrance fills the air.
　But sweeter than the lily's breath,
　And than the rose more fair,
　|:The tender love of human hearts,
　That springeth everywhere.:|

2 The rose will fade and fall away,
　The lily too will die;
　But love shall live for evermore
　Beyond the starry sky.
　Then sweeter than the lily's breath,
　And than the rose more fair,
　|:The tender love of human hearts.
　Upspringing everywhere.:|

No. 144. See the Rivers Flowing.

Tune 37.

See the rivers flowing
　Downward to the sea,
Pouring all their treasure
　Bountiful and free:
Yet to help their giving,
　Hidden springs arise;
Or, if need be, showers
　Feed them from the skies.

2 Watch the princely flowers
　Their rich fragrance spread,
Load the air with perfumes
　From their bounty shed.

Yet their lavish spending
　Leaves them not in dearth,
With fresh life replenished
　By their mother earth!

3 Give thy heart's best treasure
　From fair Nature learn;
Give thy love and ask not,
　Wait not a return;
And the more thou spendest
　From thy little store,
With a double bounty
　God will give the more.

No. 145. A Mother's Love.

1 Hast thou sounded the depths of yonder sea?
Hast thou counted the sands that under it be?
Hast thou measured the height of heaven above?
Then mayest thou speak of a mother's love.

2 Hast thou gone with the traveller, near or far
From pole to pole, from star to star?
Thou hast; and, on earth or river or sea,
The heart of a mother has gone with thee.

3 There is not a grand inspiring thought,
There is not a truth by wisdom taught,
There is not a feeling pure and high,
That may not be read in a mother's eye.

Services and Responses.

FIRST SERVICE.
Hymn.
Responses.

O **Come** let us sing unto the Lord, let us heartily rejoice in the rock of our salvation:

[*All singing:*]

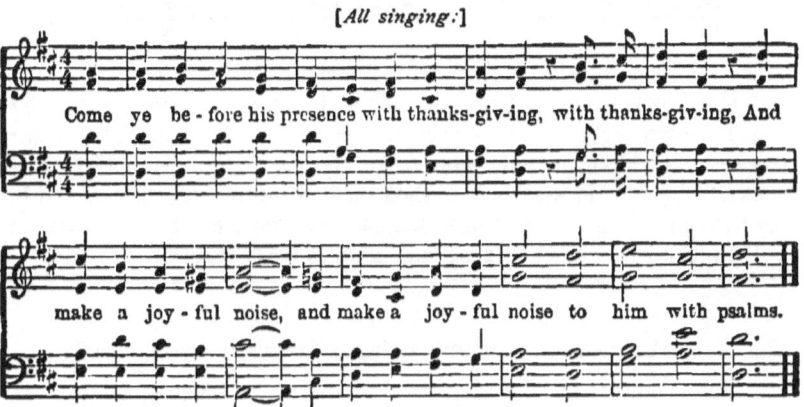

Come ye be-fore his presence with thanks-giv-ing, with thanks-giv-ing, And make a joy-ful noise, and make a joy-ful noise to him with psalms.

In his hands are the depths of the earth; his also are the heights of the mountains.

[*All singing—music as before.*]

The mighty sea is his and he hath made it;
It is his hand that formeth the dry land.

O come, let us worship and bow down, let us bow down before the Lord, our Maker!

[*All singing—music as before.*]

Come ye before his presence with thanksgiving,
And make a joyful noise to him with psalms.

For he is our God, and we are the people of his pasture and the flock of his hand.

[*The School will stand.*]

Praised be the Lord, to whom all praise is due!

[*All singing:*]

Bo-ruch A-do-noy ha'm' vo-roch-l'-o-lom vo-ed.

[*All read in unison:*]

We Praise thee, O Lord, our God, Ruler of the universe, who in thy mercy causest light to shine over the earth and all its inhabitants, and renewest daily in kindness the wonders of creation. How manifold are thy works, O Eternal; in wisdom hast thou made them all; the earth is full of thy treasures. Thou formest light and darkness, ordainest the good and the evil, bringest harmony into nature, and peace to the heart of man. AMEN.

Responses.

Our portion has fallen to us in lovely places; we have a goodly inheritance.

Moses commanded us a law, the inheritance of the congregation of Israel.

The law of the Lord is perfect, restoring the soul:

    It is a tree of life to those who lay hold of it, and the supporters thereof are happy.

Its ways are ways of pleasantness;

    And all its paths are peace.

Therefore let us joyfully lift up our voices together and proclaim the unity of God: Hear, O Israel, the Eternal is our God, the Eternal is one.

[*All singing:*]

Sh'ma Yis-ro-el A-do-noy E-lo-he-nu A-do-noy E-chod.

Responses.

Eternal Truth is thy word unto us: Thou alone art our God, there is none besides thee.

And we are thy people Israel, whom thou hast redeemed from the power of tyrants.

Wonders without number hast thou wrought for us, and hast graciously protected us to this day.

Thou hast destined our soul unto life, and hast not suffered our feet to stumble.

Thy love has watched over us in the night of oppression,

And thy mercy has sustained us in the hour of trial.

And now that we live in a land of freedom, may we still cling faithfully to thee and thy word.

O Lord, give unto thy people a pure heart, that they may serve thee with one accord.

Lead us, O Lord, in thy truth, may thy kindness preserve us ever-more.

May thy love rule over all thy children, and thy truth unite them in the bonds of fellowship.

Who is like thee among the mighty, O God! who is like thee resplendent in holiness, in awe-inspiring power, in deeds of wonder!

[*All singing:*]

Mi - cho - mo - cho bo - e - lim A - do - noy. Mi - cho - mo - cho - ne - e - dor - bak-ko-desh no - ro, s'hil - los o - sch fe - lch.

As our fathers of old proclaimed thy kingdom of justice, love, and truth, so do we to-day declare: God reigneth for ever and ever:

[*All singing:*]

A - do - noy yim - loch l' o - lom - vo - ed.

[*The school will stand and read in unison:*]

Our Heavenly Father, let thy blessing of peace rest upon us and give us strength. Help us to follow the voice of conscience and to obey thy laws cheerfully. May we love the truth and speak the truth. May we be kind to one another, tender-hearted and forgiving, holding no anger nor malice, nor speaking ill of any one. May the thought of thee keep us from doing any evil. Inspire us with humility, with faith and trust in thee. Bless our parents and our teachers and all those who are engaged in good and noble works. AMEN.

[*All singing:*]

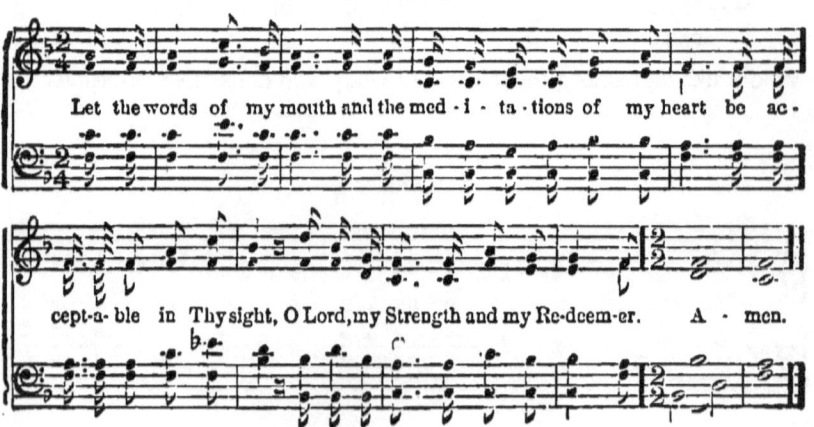

Let the words of my mouth and the med-i-ta-tions of my heart be ac-cept-a-ble in Thy sight, O Lord, my Strength and my Re-deem-er. A - men.

Scripture Reading, or Address.

Class Lessons.

Hymn.

Dismissal.

SECOND SERVICE.

Hymn.

Responses:

Raise a voice of joy unto the Lord, all ye lands! serve the Lord with gladness; come before his presence with songs!

Know ye that the Eternal is God! it is he that made us, and we are his people, and the flock of his pasture.

[All singing—music as above.]

Praise ye the Lord, who with majesty ruleth in all things;
Who thee preserves and upbears as on pinions of eagles;
Who thee upholds when by thyself thou wouldst fall.
Verily, hast thou not known it?

Enter into his courts with praise; be thankful to him and bless his name!

[All singing—music as above.]

Praise ye the Lord, and behold with thine eyes all his mercies;
Out of the heavens his love raineth like unto rivers.
Think, O thou man, what is the might of his hand.
Who daily meets thee with blessings.

For the Lord is good; his mercy is everlasting; and his truth endureth to all generations.

Sanctification.

We will sanctify the name of the Holy One of Israel, as it is **sanctified** throughout the universe; and in the solemn words of our prophets proclaim: Holy, holy, holy is the Lord of hosts, the whole world is full of his glory.

[*All singing:*]

Ko - dosh, ko - dosh, ko - dosh A - do - noy Ts' - vo - os m'lo chol ho - o - rets k' - vo - do.

Praised be the glory of God in all places of his dominion.

[*All singing:*]

Bo - ruch k' - vod A - do - noy mi - m' - ko - mo.

The Lord shall reign forever, thy God, O Zion, to all generations, Hallelujah.

[*All singing:*]

Yim - loch A - do - noy l'o - lom e - lo - ha yich Tsi - on l'

Responses.

Thou Shalt love the Eternal, thy God, with all thy heart, with all thy soul, and with all thy might.

It hath been told to thee, O man, what is good and what the **Lord** doth require of thee: to do justly, to love virtue, and to walk humbly with thy God.

Prayer.

[All read in unison.]

O Thou Creator of all worlds! the earth is full of thy bounty. On all sides, above and beneath, are the proofs of thy wisdom and power. All thy works praise thee; and the whole creation tells of thy lovingkindness. May we also praise thee and love thee. May the sun remind us of thy glory, the moon and the stars at night of thy care. May the rain that falleth alike on the evil and the good assure us of thy bounty. May the fruits of the earth that nourish us, quicken us to feel and acknowledge thy fatherly care; so that thou mayest be in all our thoughts. And enjoying so much at thy hand, may we seek to imitate thy love and goodness, by doing good to all around us. AMEN.

Scripture Reading, or Address.
Hymn.
Class Lessons.
Hymn.
Benediction.

[All unite.]

May the Lord bless us and keep us. The Lord make his face to shine upon us, and be gracious unto us. The Lord lift up the light of his countenance upon us, and give us peace. AMEN.

THIRD SERVICE.
Hymn.

Responses:

(Psalm 96.)

O Sing unto the Lord a new song; sing unto the Lord all the earth; sing unto the Lord, bless his name: show forth his salvation from day to day.

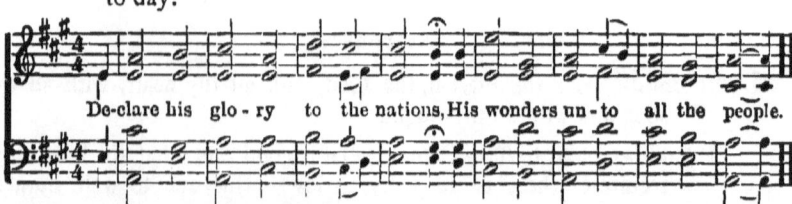

De-clare his glo-ry to the nations, His wonders un-to all the people.

Glory and majesty are before him; strength and beauty are in his sanctuary.
O worship him in holy beauty,
With reverence worship, all the earth.

Say among the nations, The Lord reigneth: the world also is stablished that it cannot be moved; he shall judge the people in righteousness.

Ye heavens be glad, and earth be joyful,
The sea and all its fullness roar.

Let the field exult and all that is therein: then shall all the trees of the wood sing for joy before the Lord; for he cometh, he cometh to judge the earth.

The world with righteousness he judgeth,
And all the people with his truth.

(Psalm 92.)

It is good to give thanks to the Lord, and to sing praises to thy name, O Most High!
To show forth thy lovingkindness in the morning, and thy faithfulness every night.

For thou, O Lord, hast made me glad by thy doings;
In the works of thy hands I greatly rejoice!

How great are thy works, O Lord! how deep thy purposes!
But the unwise man knoweth not this, the thoughtless can not perceive it,

When the wicked spring up like grass, and evil-doers flourish;—to be destroyed for ever!

The righteous shall flourish like the palm-tree; they shall grow up like the cedars of Lebanon.

Planted in the house of the Lord, they shall flourish in the courts of our God.

Even in old age they bring forth fruit: they are green, and full of sap;

To show that the Lord, my rock, is upright, and there is no unrighteousness in him.

[*All singing:*]

It is good to render to the Lord thanksgiving, And to sing to the Lord with praise, And to sing to the Lord with praise.

To declare his loving-kindness in the morning: And his faithfulness every night.

[*All read in unison.*]

With infinite love hast thou guided our fathers, O Lord, our God! They trusted in thee, and thou didst teach them the laws of life. O be gracious unto us; incline our hearts to thee, merciful Father! Enlighten our minds that we may understand the truth; purify our hearts that we may love the good; prompt our will that our deeds may never put us to shame. In thy holy name we put our trust; we rejoice and delight in thy help.

Eternal, our God, and God of our fathers, Almighty Ruler of the universe, who renderest just recompense unto all thy creatures; eternal is thy love, as thy might is infinite. Thou sustainest in mercy the living, thou upholdest the falling, healest the sick, freest the imprisoned, and fulfillest thy gracious promise to those who sleep in the dust. Blessed art thou, O God, perfect in justice and holiness.

[*The School will stand.*]

We bow the head and bend the knee before the Ruler of the world, and praise his holy name.

Va - a - nach - nu ko - r' - im u - mish-tach - a - vim u - mo - dim. lif-ne me - lech ma l'che ha-m'-lo chim hak - ko - dosh boruch hu.

The Lord shall be King over all the earth; on that day shall the Lord be acknowledged one, and his name shall be one.

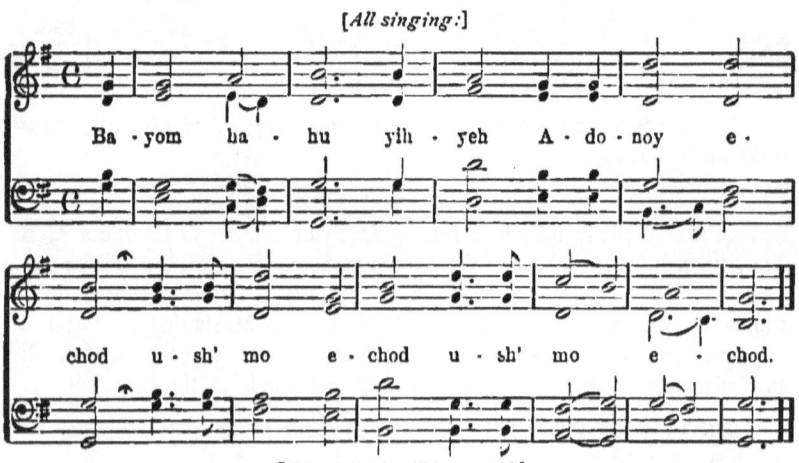

Ba - yom ha - hu yih - yeh A - do - noy e - chod u - sh' mo e - chod u - sh' mo e - chod.

[*The School will be seated.*]

Scripture Reading, or Address.

Class Lessons.

Hymn.

FOURTH SERVICE.

Hymn.

Responses.

(Psalm 84.)

How lovely are thy tabernacles, O Lord of hosts!
My soul longeth for the courts of the Lord;
My heart and my flesh cry aloud for the living God.

Happy are they who dwell in thy house, they will continually praise thee!
Happy the man whose glory is in thee, in whose heart are thy ways!

They go on from strength to strength; every one of them appeareth before God in Zion.

Hear my prayer, O Lord, God of hosts! give ear, O God of Jacob!

For a day spent in thy courts is better than a thousand without:

I would rather stand on the threshold of the house of my God, than dwell in the tents of wickedness.

For the Lord God is a sun and a shield; the Lord giveth grace and glory;
No good thing doth he withold from those who walk uprightly.

O Lord of hosts! happy the man who trusteth in thee!

[*All singing:*]

Let the words of my mouth and the med-i-ta-tion of my heart be ac-cept-a-ble in thy sight O Lord my Strength and my Re-deem-er.

(Psalm 103.)

Bless the Lord, O my soul! and all that is within me, bless his holy name!
Bless the Lord, O my soul, and forget not all his benefits.
Who forgiveth all thine iniquities and healeth all thy diseases.
The Lord is gracious and kind, slow to anger and rich in mercy.
As high as are the heavens above the earth, so great is his mercy to them that fear him.

[*All singing:*]

Like as a fa-ther pit-ieth his chil-dren,
The Lord pit-ieth them that fear him.

For he knoweth our frame, he remembereth that we are dust.
As for man, his days are as grass; as the flower of the field, so he flourisheth.
The wind passeth over it, and it is gone; and its place shall know it no more.
But the mercy of the Lord is from everlasting to everlasting to them that fear him, and his righteousness to children's children.

[*All singing—music as before.*]

To them that keep his commandments.
That keep his commandments to do them.
Bless the Lord, O my soul! his kingdom ruleth over all.
Bless the Lord, all ye his hosts; ye, his ministers, who obey his will!
Bless the Lord, all his works, in all places of his dominion!

[*All singing—music as before.*]

Bless ye the Lord his works in all places,
All places of his dominion.

[*All read in unison:*]

We thank thee, O God, for the return of the morning and the renewal of our daily blessings. We love to feel that we are always surrounded by thee, and that the blessings of each day are the gifts of thy providence. We love to feel that thou art coming to us in the morning air and sunshine, the evening's calm, in the love of our loved ones, in our work and our play, and in all things that make us glad and strong. May all that is beautiful remind us of thee, the infinite beauty. May all that is good remind us of thee, the perfect goodness. May all that is true lead us to thee, the source of truth. AMEN.

[*All singing:*]

Ho-ly! Ho-ly! Ho-ly! Lord of Hosts! Ho-ly! Ho-ly! Ho-ly! Lord of Hosts! Heav'n and earth are full of the maj-es-ty, the maj-es-ty of thy great glo-ry.

Scripture Reading, or Address.

Hymn.

Class Lessons.

Hymn.

Benediction.

FIFTH SERVICE.

Hymn.

Responses.

(Psalm 121.)

I will lift up mine eyes unto the hills. From whence cometh my help? My help cometh from the Lord who made heaven and earth.

[All singing:]

He will not let thy foot be moved, He will not slumber, not slum-ber.

Lo, he that keeps thee, Lo, he that keeps thee, Slumbers not nor sleeps.

The Lord is thy keeper; the Lord is thy shade upon thy right hand.

The sun shall not smite thee by day, nor the moon by night.

The Lord shall keep thee from all evil. He shall keep thy soul.

[All singing—music as above.]

The Lord shall keep thy going out
And thy incoming, incoming;.
From this time forth,
From this time forth, and
Even for evermore.

(Psalms 112, 41 and 1.)

Happy the man who feareth the Lord, who taketh delight in his commandments!

To the righteous shall arise light out of darkness; and happy the man who is pitiful and kind, he shall sustain his cause in judgment;

The righteous shall be in everlasting remembrance.

He is not afraid of evil tidings; his heart is firm, trusting in the Lord.

He hath scattereth blessings; he giveth to the poor.

His righteousness shall endure forever.

Happy are they who have regard to justice, who practice righteousness at all times!

Happy is he who hath regard to the poor! the Lord will deliver him in time of trouble.

The Lord will preserve him, and keep him alive; he shall be happy on the earth.

Happy the man who walketh not in the counsel of the unrighteous.

Nor standeth in the way of sinners, nor sitteth in the seat of scoffers;

But whose delight is in the law of the Lord.

And who meditateth on his precepts day and night.

He is like a tree planted by streams of water, that bringeth forth its fruit in its reason,

Whose leaves also do not wither; all that he doeth shall prosper,

Not so the unrighteous; they are like chaff, which the wind driveth away.

Therefore the wicked shall not stand in judgment,

Nor sinners in the assembly of the just.

For the Lord knoweth the way of the righteous;

But the way of the wicked leadeth to ruin.

[*All singing:*]

Worship the Lord in the beauty of holiness, Worship the Lord in the beauty of holiness; Fear before him all the earth.

[*All read in unison.*]

O Thou, Eternal One, we thank thee for the signs and tokens of thyself which thou hast placed around us everywhere. We thank thee for this new day, for the broad earth beneath our feet, for the wonderful heavens above our heads. We thank thee that all these things teach us of thee. They tell us of thy greatness; they speak of thy wisdom, and talk of thy power. But more than in all these things thou speakest to us in thy still small voice which whispers in our souls. We thank thee that there thou hast written that thou art our Father, and that thy name is Love. May we always feel thy presence around us and within us, and love the things that thou lovest, and serve thee with the service of our daily lives. AMEN.

[*All singing:*]

Scripture Reading, or Address.

Class Lessons.

Hymn.

SIXTH SERVICE.

Hymn.

Responses.

The Heavens declare the glory of God, and the firmament showeth his handiwork:

Day unto day uttereth speech, and night unto night showeth knowledge.

There is no speech nor language; their voice cannot be heard:

Yet their-line is gone out through all the earth, and their words to the end of the world.

In them hath he set a tabernacle for the sun, which is as a bridegroom coming out of his chamber and rejoiceth as a strong man to run a race:

His going forth is from the end of the heavens and his circuit unto the ends of it, and there is nothing hid from the heat thereof.

The law of the Lord is perfect, restoring the soul:

The testimony of the Lord is sure, making wise the simple:

The precepts of the Lord are right, rejoicing the heart:

The commandment of the Lord is pure, enlightening the eyes:

The fear of the Lord is clean, enduring forever; the judgments of the Lord are true and righteous altogether:

More to be desired are they than gold, yea, than much fine gold; sweeter also than honey and the honeycomb:

Moreover by them is thy servant warned:

In keeping of them there is a great reward.

Who can discern his errors? Cleanse thou me from hidden faults:

Keep back thy servant also from presumptuous sins. Let them not have dominion over me.

Then shall I be upright, and I shall be innocent from great transgression:

[*All singing—music page 126.*]

Let the words of my mouth and the meditation of my heart be acceptable in thy sight, O Lord, my Strength and my Redeemer.

[*All read in unison:*]

Our God and Father! all living creatures praise and glorify thy name, and all men bow down before thee in worship and gratitude. From eternity to eternity thou art God, who supportest, preservest, and savest us mercifully in times of need and affliction. From beginning to end thou art the Lord of all creation.

Responses.

(Psalm 139.)

O Lord! thou hast searched me and known me!

Thou knowest my sitting-down and my rising-up;

Thou understandest my thoughts from afar!

Thou seest my path and my lying-down, and art acquainted with all my ways!

For before the word is upon my tongue, behold, O Lord! thou knowest it altogether!

Thou hast beset me behind and before, and laid thy hand upon me.

Such knowledge is too wonderful for me; it is high; I cannot attain to it!

[*All singing:*]

Where shall I go from thy spir-it, Where shall I go from thy spir-it? Whith-er from thy pres-ence flee?

If I ascend into heaven, thou art there.

If I make my bed in the underworld, behold, thou art there!

If I take the wings of the morning, and dwell in remotest parts of the sea.

[*All singing—music as above.*]

Even there shall thy hand lead me,

And thy right hand shall hold me!

If I say, Surely the darkness shall cover me; even the night shall be light about me.

[*All singing—music as before.*]

Yea, the darkness hideth not from thee,
But the night shineth as the day.

The darkness and the light are both alike to thee!

I will praise thee; for I am wonderfully made;

Marvelous are thy works, and this my soul knoweth full well!

Thine eyes did see my substance, while yet unformed, and in thy book was everything written;

My days were appointed before one of them existed.

How precious to me are thy thoughts, O God! how great is the sum of them!

If I should count them, they would outnumber the sand; when I awake, I am still with thee!

Search me, O God! and know my heart; try me, and know my thoughts;

[*All singing—music as before.*]

See if there be evil in me.
Lead me in thy holy way.

[*All read in unison.*]

O thou who givest the day for labor and the night for rest, we lift our hearts to thee. Thou veilest the face of nature and all is still: thou speakest to us in the soft twilight. The very silence hymns thy praise. Thou leadest forth the stars, and callest them all by their names. Thou art in the shadow that closes around us, and in the day-spring that wakes us again. Whither can we go from thy Spirit, and whither can we flee from thy presence? May the eye that never slumbers watch over us in our waking and in our sleep. Make us to know thy lovingkindness, O Lord, in the morning, and strengthen us for the duties of the morrow. AMEN.

[*All singing:*]

Be it good for us to be here:

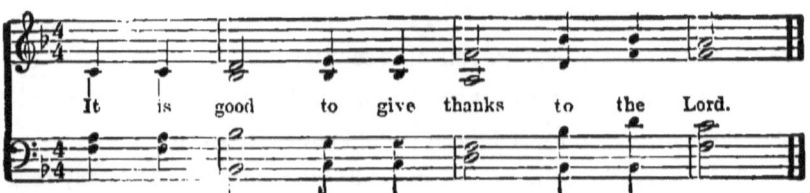

Be this house Peace:

To do his will from the heart:

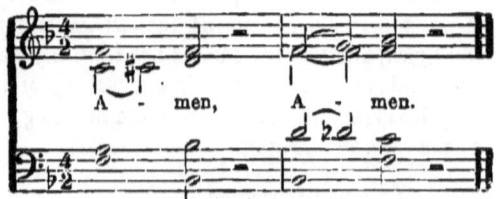

Scripture Reading, or Address.
Hymn.
Class Lessons
Hymn.
Dismissal.

The Flower Service.

Organ.

Processional.

Hymn or Anthem.

Peace be on this house; peace and joy to every soul therein.

[*All singing:*]

A - men, A - men, Hal - le - lu - jah!

The Eternal goodness of God giveth great beauty to the earth and gladness to the heart; for as his majesty so is his mercy.

[*All singing:*]

A - men, Hal - le - lu - jah!

O Lord, how manifold are thy works! In wisdom hast thou made them all; the earth is full of thy riches.

[*All singing:*]

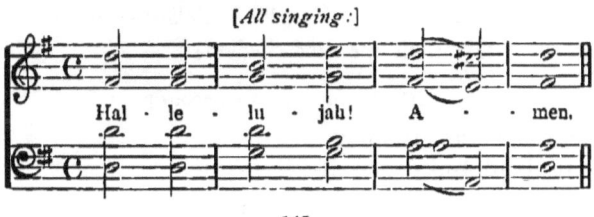

Hal - le - lu - jah! A - men.

Responses.

Beauty is spread upon the hills, and the valleys are full of flowers.

Wonderful is the life of Nature that shows forth the glory of God.

Yet this earthly beauty is but a little of that which is in store.

No one can measure the riches of God.

Eye hath not seen nor ear heard the things that God hath prepared for those that serve him.

(Psalm 148.)

Praise ye the Lord! praise the Lord from the heavens! praise him in the heights.

Praise ye him, sun and moon! praise him, all ye stars of light!

Let them praise the name of the Lord; for he commanded, and they were created.

[All singing—music as above.]

Praise the Lord, all ye hosts!
Hallelujah, Amen.

Praise the Lord from the earth, ye sea-monsters, and all deeps!

Ye mountains, and all hills! fruit trees and all cedars!

Ye wild beasts, and all cattle! ye creeping things, and winged birds!

Ye kings, and all peoples, princes, and all judges of the earth!

Young men and maidens, old men and children!

[All singing—music as above.]

O give thanks with glad song:
Praise the Lord, Amen! Amen!

Let them praise the name of the Lord! for his name alone is exalted;

His glory is above the earth and the heavens.

He lifteth up the glory of his children, and exalteth those that are near unto him. Praise ye the Lord!

[*All singing—music as before.*]

Praise the Lord, all ye hosts!
Hallelujah, Amen.

Responses.

Lo, the winter is over and gone; the flowers appear again on the earth;

The time of the singing of the birds has come and the voice of the dove is heard in our land.

The orchards put forth their green fruit, and the vines are fragrant with tender grapes.

The cold came out of the north; by the breath of God the frost was given.

The dust grew into hardness, and the clods cleaved fast together.

The waters were hid as with a stone, and the face of the deep was frozen.

Thou sendest out thy word and meltest them; thou causest thy wind to blow and the waters flow.

Thou visitest the earth and waterest it; thou waterest the hills thereof abundantly;

Thou sendest rain into the valleys and makest them soft with showers;

Thou satisfiest the desolate ground and blessest the springing thereof.

Wherefore if God so clothe the grass of the field, will he not much more care for his children?

The grass withereth, the flower fadeth, but the word of the Lord endureth forever.

Anthem or Hymn.

Scripture Reading.

Address or Recitations.

Hymn.

The Good and the Beautiful.

[To be recited by one of the pupils.]

O Painter of the fruits and flowers,
We own thy wise design,
Whereby these human hands of ours
May share the works of thine!

Apart from thee, we plant in vain
The root, and sow the seed;
Thy early and thy latter rain,
Thy sun and dew we need.

Why search the wide world everywhere,
For Eden's unknown ground?—
That garden of the primal pair
May never more be found.

But, blest by thee, our patient toil
May right the ancient wrong,
And give to every clime and soil
The beauty lost so long.

Its earliest shrines the young world sought,
In hill-groves, and in bowers;
The fittest offerings thither brought,
Were thy own fruits and flowers.

And still with reverent hands we cull
Thy gifts, each year renewed;
The good is always beautiful,
The beautiful is good.

Prayer.

[*All read in unison:*]

O Lord of heaven and earth, we bless thee for thy gracious bounty! In this summer season of fulness and plenty, thou dost scatter thy blessings with an open hand, making even the waysides and lonely places rich with beauty. Thou art our Father; and with the reverence and wonder of adoring children, we behold thy works and seek to know thy ways. Thy life gives to the flowers their grace and their beauty; and we hear thy voice in the songs of the birds, in the gentle breezes, and the flowing waters. May we gain a double blessing from this festival of flowers,—the blessing of beauty, and the blessing of holy teaching! Gracious Father! there are flowers that may be opened within our hearts,—fair blossoms of fidelity, and charity, and peace. Shine upon us by thy light, that these graces of character may give forth their fragrance. May no outward thing pass from our sight till it has filled our minds with some new lesson of wisdom and of goodness. AMEN.

Organ Voluntary.

Flower-Offering.

The class offerings are baskets or bunches of flowers, or of other emblems of Summer, brought to the pulpit by one child from each class of the Sabbath School, or by all of each class if desired. Each offering should contain some appropriate verse or sentence written on paper, which may be taken out and read by the minister as he receives the offering; then the offerings should be placed one after the other on the pulpit or on a table placed for the purpose. There may be a verse of a song or a chant after each offering, by the children or choir. This pretty and cheerful custom may be much varied and enjoyed in many different ways, according to the taste or convenience of any congregation that makes them, to join with the hands and voices of the children in celebrating the beauty and blessing of the Summer. After the exercises the offerings should be sent to one of the hospitals or other charitable institutions of the city.

Closing Benediction.

The Harvest Service.

Organ.　Anthem or Hymn.

𝔓eace be on this house; peace and joy to every soul therein.

[All singing:]

A - men,　A - men,　Hal - le - lu - jah!

𝔈nter into these gates with thanksgiving and into these courts with praise!

[All singing:]

A - men,　Hal - le - lu - jah!

𝔉or the Lord is good; his mercy is everlasting; and his truth endureth to all generations.

[All singing:]

Hal - le - lu - jah!　A - - men.

Responses.

Holy and joyful is the festival of the Harvest:

The showers have come down in their season; there have been showers of blessings.

The tree hath yielded its fruit, and the earth its increase;

And we have been safe in the land.

The summer is past, the harvest is come: now is the ingathering of the year.

The sons of men go forth to their labor, and the land yieldeth for them food.

In the fields they reap the harvest, and gather the vintage from the vineyard.

The hills are girded with gladness and the pastures are clothed with flocks.

Blessed of God is the land for the dew of heaven and for the deep that sleepeth beneath;

For the precious fruits brought forth by the sun, and for the precious things put forth by the rain;

For the precious things of the earth and its fullness, and for the good will of him who giveth all.

Then let the fields be joyful, and all that is therein.

The Lord crowneth the year with his goodness; the earth is full of his riches.

(Psalm 104.)

Bless the Lord, O my soul! O Lord, my God! thou art very great! Thou art clothed with glory and majesty!

[All singing:]

Who cov-er-est thy-self with light, With light as with a gar-ment;

Who stretchest out a-far the heavens, Them like a cur-tain stretch-est.

He sendeth forth the springs in brooks; they run among the mountains;
> About them the birds of heaven have their habitation; they sing among the branches.

He watereth the hills from his clouds; the earth is satisfied with the fruit of thy works!

> *[All singing—music as before.]*
>
> The grass to grow up doth he cause,
> To grow up for the cattle;
> And every herb to nourish man,
> Who from the earth food bringeth.

He appointed the moon to mark seasons; the sun knoweth when to go down.
> Man goeth forth to his work, and to his labor, until the evening.

> *[All singing—music as before.]*
>
> O Lord how manifold are thy works—
> In wisdom hast thou made them;
> In wisdom hast thou made them all.
> The earth is full of riches.

All thy creatures, innumerable, wait upon thee, that thou mayest give them their food in due season.
> Thou givest it to them, they gather it; thou openest thy hand, they are atisfied with good.

Thou hidest thy face, they are confounded; thou takest away their breath, they die, and return to the dust.
> Thou sendest forth thy spirit, they are created, and thou renewest the face of the earth.

The glory of the Lord shall endure forever; the Lord rejoiceth in his works.
> May my meditation be acceptable to him! I will rejoice in the Lord.

Bless the Lord, O my soul! praise ye the Lord!

> *[All singing—music as before.]*
>
> Now will I sing unto the Lord,
> And while I live sing ever;
> Praise will I sing unto my God
> As long as I have being.

𝕷et us acknowledge the goodness which fills the earth with food;
   Food for the body, and food for the souls of God's creatures,—
The glory of knowledge, the light of religion,
   The strength that comes in time of need,
The faith and peace that follow sorrow.
   O let us be filled with joyful thanksgiving,
And all that is within us bless his holy name.
   Wherefore, with one accord, let us raise a voice of joy to God,
Coming before his presence with rejoicing,
   And singing praises from the heart.

[*All singing:*]
(Psalm cxlv.)

Sing praise un-to the Lord with thanks-giv-ing: Sing praise un-to the Lord with thanks-giv-ing: The Lord upholdeth all that fall, and raiseth them that are bowed down: Sing praise un-to the Lord......... with thanks-giv-ing.

[*All read in unison.*]

𝔓raised forever be thy name who art our Father. Thou art the Lord, mighty and holy in heaven and on earth. Song and praise, hymn and music, might and dominion, eternity, greatness and power, adoration and glory, holiness and majesty, benedictions and thanksgivings are thine, thine forever and ever. AMEN.

[*All singing:*]

Psalm 66.

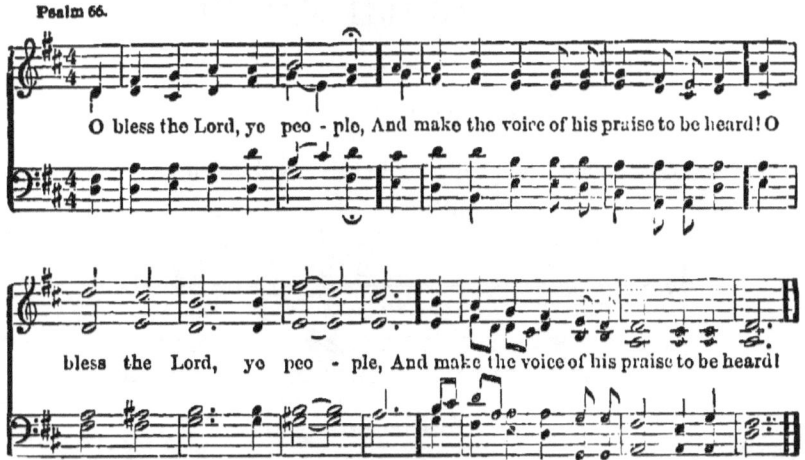

O bless the Lord, ye peo-ple, And make the voice of his praise to be heard! O bless the Lord, ye peo-ple, And make the voice of his praise to be heard!

Our soul in life he holdeth: And suff'reth never our feet to be moved.

[*All read in unison.*]

We praise thee, O thou Source of all life and strength and blessing, for the bountiful provision which thou makest for the wants of thy children, filling the earth with food and our hearts with gladness. We would bring thee now our joyful thanksgiving for the harvest of the fields. Thou hast ordered the course of the changing seasons, and appointed a time for sowing and a time for reaping; and while men have toiled, or watched, or rested from their work, thy providence has never failed, and thou hast prepared for them the reward of their labors. May we enjoy the gifts of thy bounty in wisdom, temperance, and thankfulness, ever mindful of the love which bestowed them. And may the remembrance of thy fatherly goodness to us make our thoughts kind and gracious towards all our brethren whom we may help and cheer; that we may be ever generous, kind and considerate, ready to succor the needy and feed the hungry, and rejoicing to lighten any burden of poverty and distress.

Scripture Reading.

Hymn.

Sermon.

Patriotic Hymn.

Conclusion, page 163.

The National Service.

Organ. Anthem or Hymn.

𝔓eace be on this house; peace and joy to every soul therein.

Responses.

𝕮he earth is the Lord's, and all that is therein; the world and they who inhabit it.

For he hath founded it upon the seas, and established it upon the floods.

Who shall ascend the hill of the Lord? and who shall stand in his holy place?

He that hath clean hands and a pure heart;

Who hath not inclined his soul to falsehood, nor sworn deceitfully.

He shall receive a blessing from the Lord, and favor from the God of his salvation.

This is the race of those that seek thee; those that seek thy face, O God.

𝔅eautiful is the dawn, ushering in the new-born day,—

Renewing the face of the earth, quickening all things to life:

But fairer than the morning's light is the light of noble memories,

Renewing within us the springs of holy feeling and thought,

Speaking of country and home, and binding the generations in one.

Put on thy beautiful garments, O land,

Gird thee for gladness, sing aloud for joy!

Gather thy people, gather them all unto thee.

That they may keep thy Festival, the day thou ordainest to hallow.

From thy hill-sides and valleys,
From thy well-tilled fields and thy busy marts,
From the workshop and the mill, the forge and the loom,
From the halls of council, and learning's quiet retreats,
Gather thy people, gather them all unto thee:
They shall all be one in thee this day,—
In thee, our Country, the land of our loyalty and love.

Hymn.

[These lines may be sung as an anthem by the choir or read as responses.]

Lift up your heads, O ye gates! lift yourselves up, ye everlasting doors, that the King of glory may come!

"Who is this King of glory?" The Lord, strong and mighty; the Lord, mighty in battle.

Lift up your heads, O ye gates! lift yourselves up, ye everlasting doors, that the King of glory may enter in!

"Who is this King of glory?" The Lord, God of hosts, he is the King of glory.

Scripture Prayer.

O God, we have heard with our ears, our fathers have told us, what deeds thou didst in their days, what thou didst in the days of old. With a strong hand, and an outstretched arm thou didst guide the people across the sea; thou didst scatter the inhabitants before them, and didst cause our fathers to prosper. Not by their swords obtained they the land, nor did their own arms give them the victory; but thy right hand and thine arm, because thou hadst favor unto them. When they went from nation to nation, from one kingdom to another people, thou didst suffer no man to turn them; thou didst reprove kings for their sakes, when they were yet very few in number, very few and strangers in the land; when they were wandering in the wilderness, and found no city to dwell in; when they were hungry and thirsty, and their souls grew faint within them, then they cried unto the Lord in their trouble, and thou deliverest them out of all their distresses. The little one hath become a thousand, and the small one a great nation: let the redeemed of the Lord say this whom he hath redeemed from many lands: from the east and from the west, and from the north and from the south. O let us praise the Lord for his goodness, for his wonderful works to the children of men. Our portion hath fallen to us in pleasant places; yea, we have a goodly heritage. The Lord our God be with us, as he was with our fathers: that he may incline our hearts unto him to keep his commandments, and to walk in his ways. AMEN.

Responses.

Blessed is the nation whose God is the Lord; the people that he hath chosen for his inheritance.

Open ye the gates that the righteous nation may enter in.

For when the righteous are in authority the people rejoice;

But when the wicked bear rule the people mourn.

Blessed art thou, O land, when thy law is not slackened;

When thou makest thy rulers righteousness, and thine officers peace;

When each despiseth the gain of oppression, and shaketh his hands from holding bribes;

When he respecteth not the person of the poor, nor honoreth the person of the mighty;

But in righteousness serveth the people, and establisheth true judgment in thy gates.

Then shall violence be no more heard in thy land, wasting and destruction within thy borders.

Then shall justice roll down as waters, and righteousness as a mighty stream.

And thou shalt call thy walls Salvation and thy gates Praise.

For righteousness exalteth a nation and injustice is a reproach to any people.

And in righteousness hath the Lord called thee and given thee for a light to the kingdoms.

O God, we have heard with our ears, and our fathers have told us,

What works thou didst in their days, and in the old times before them.

Our lines have fallen unto us in pleasant places, yea we have a goodly heritage.

O give thanks unto the Lord, for he is good, for his mercy endureth forever.

And pray for the peace of our country; all they shall prosper who love thee.

[*All read in unison:*]

Lord, thou hast been our dwelling-place in all generations. In thee our fathers trusted; they trusted and were not dismayed. In thee their souls abide, their bodies are buried in peace. Be thou to their children guidance and strength. Thanks be to thee for the heritage to which we are called. Blessed be thy name for the memories of the good, the examples of faithful lives, the stored wisdom from devout and diligent minds, the steadfast faith and patient labor of those who have made the earth more beautiful for us who follow them. Pilgrims and sojourners are we as all our fathers were. Give us grace to live worthily, to hold our inheritance as a sacred trust, that we may leave it with increase for those who shall come after. AMEN.

Responses.

Let us call to remembrance the great and good, through whom the Lord hath wrought great glory.

Those who were leaders of the people by their judgment;

Those who gave counsel by their understanding and foresight.

Wise and eloquent in their teachings, and through knowledge and might fit helpers of the people.

All these were honored in their generation, and were the glory of their times.

There be some who have left a name behind them; whose remembrance is sweet as honey in all mouths.

And there be some who have no memorial; who are perished as though they had never been.

But their righteousness has not been forgotten, and the glory of their work cannot be blotted out.

Their bodies are buried in peace, but their name liveth for evermore.

The people will tell of their wisdom, and the congregation will show forth their praise.

For the memorial virtue is immortal; because it is known with God and with men.

When it is present, mankind take example of it, and when it is gone, they earnestly desire for it.

It weareth a crown, and triumpheth forever, having gotten the victory striving for undefiled rewards.

The righteous shall be in everlasting remembrance and the memory of the just shall be blessed.

Though a good life hath but few days, yet a good name endureth forever.

Though the righteous be overtaken by death, they shall be at rest, their souls are in the hand of God.

Though they vanish from the sight of men, yet is their hope full of immortality.

Patriotic Hymn.
Discourse, or Addresses.
Recitations, or other Exercises.
Conclusion, page 163.

'Hanukkah and Purim Service.

Organ. Processional.
Hymn.

Peace be on this house; peace and joy to every soul therein.

[*All singing:*] Hal - le - lu - jah! A - - men!

Responses.

Praise ye the Lord! For it is good to sing praises unto our God; for it is pleasant, and praise is becoming.

Great is our God, and mighty in power; his wisdom is infinite.

The Lord lifteth up the lowly; he casteth the wicked down to the ground.

[*All singing:*]

Worship the Lord in the beauty of holiness, Worship the Lord in the beauty of holiness; Fear before him all the earth.

He counteth the number of the stars, and calls them all by their names.

Sing to the Lord with thanksgiving; sing praises unto our God.

I will praise the Lord as long as I live, and worship him while I have my being.

[*All singing—music as on page 157.*]

Worship the Lord in the beauty of holiness;
Fear before him all the earth.

(Psalm 113.)

Praise ye the Lord! praise, O ye servants of the Lord! praise the name of the Lord!

Blessed be the name of the Lord, from this time forth, even forever!

From the rising of the sun to its going down, may the name of the Lord be praised!

The Lord is high above all nations; his glory is above the heavens.

He raiseth the poor from the dust, and exalteth the needy from his lowliness.

To set him among princes, even among the princes of his people.

He causeth the forsaken to dwell in her house, a joyful mother of children.

[*All singing:*]

Praise the Lord, all ye hosts! Hal - le - lu - jah, A - men!

(Psalm 118.)

O give thanks to the Lord, for he is good;
For his kindness endureth forever!

Let the house of Israel now say,
His kindness endureth forever!

Let all who fear the Lord say,
His kindness endureth forever!

I called upon the Lord in distress; he heard, and set me in a wide place.

The Lord is on my side, I will not fear; what can man do to me?

The Lord is my helper: I shall triumph over all my enemies.

It is better to trust in the Lord than to put confidence in man;

It is better to trust in the Lord than to put confidence in princes.

The Lord is my glory and my song; for to him I owe my salvation.

The voice of joy and salvation is in the habitations of the righteous.

The right hand of the Lord doeth valiantly; the right hand of the Lord is exalted.

I shall not die, but live, and declare the deeds of the Lord.

Open to me the gates of righteousness, that I may go in, and praise the Lord!

I praise thee that thou hast heard me, and hast been my salvation.

The stone which the builders rejected hath become the chief corner-stone.

This is the Lord's doing; it is marvelous in our eyes!

This is the day which the Lord hath made; let us rejoice and be glad in it.

O give thanks to the Lord, for he is good; for his kindness endureth forever.

[*All singing:*]

[*The School will stand.*]

Praised be the Lord, to whom all praise is due!

[*All singing:*]

Bo-ruch A-do-noy ham' vo-roch-l'-o-lom vo-ed.

[*All read in unison.*]

With everlasting love thou hast guided thy people, Israel, and revealed to them thy law, whose knowledge shall bless all mankind. Therefore may we constantly think of thy word and meditate on thy precepts; for thy law is the light of our life, and by walking therein have we been preserved to this day, May thy love, O God of truth, abide with us in the future as it has been with us in the past, that we may continue to proclaim thy law and the unity of thy being, before all the nations of the earth.

Responses.

Our portion has fallen to us in lovely places; we have a goodly inheritance.

Moses commanded us a law, the inheritance of the congregation of Israel.

The law of the Lord is perfect, restoring the soul:

> It is a tree of life to those who lay hold of it, and the supporters thereof are happy.

Its ways are ways of pleasantness;

> And all its paths are peace.

Therefore let us joyfully lift up our voices together and proclaim the unity of God: Hear, O Israel, the Eternal is our God, the Eternal is one.

[*All singing:*]

Sh'ma Yis-ro-el A-do-noy E-lo-he-nu A-do-noy E-chod.

Responses.

Eternal Truth is thy word unto us: Thou alone art our God, there is none besides thee.

And we are thy people Israel, whom thou hast redeemed from the power of tyrants.

Wonders without number hast thou wrought for us, and hast graciously protected us to this day.

Thou hast destined our soul unto life, and hast not suffered our feet to stumble.

Thy love has watched over us in the night of oppression,

And thy mercy has sustained us in the hour of trial.

And now that we live in a land of freedom, may we still cling faithfully to thee and thy word.

O Lord, give unto thy people a pure heart, that they may serve thee with one accord.

Lead us, O Lord, in thy truth, may thy kindness preserve us ever-more.

May thy love rule over all thy children, and thy truth unite them in the bonds of fellowship.

Who is like thee among the mighty, O God! who is like thee resplendent in holiness, in awe-inspiring power, in deeds of wonder!

[*All singing:*]

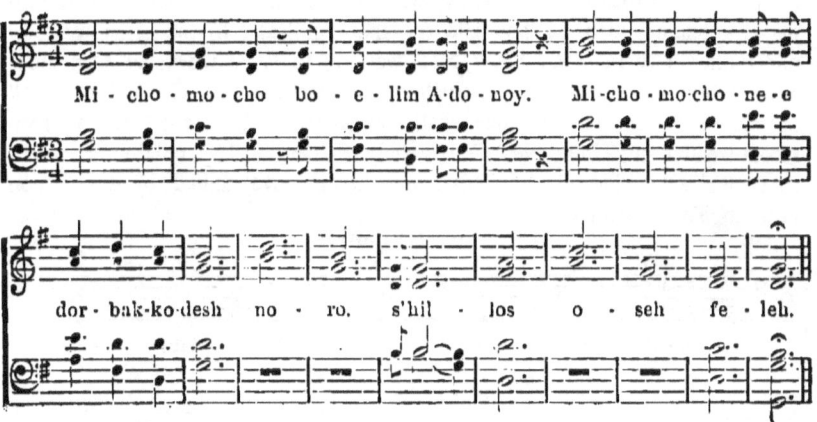

Mi - cho - mo - cho bo - e - lim A-do - noy. Mi - cho - mo-cho - ne - e dor - bak-ko-desh no - ro. s'hi - los o - seh fe - leh.

[*The School will stand.*]
For Hanukkah.

We thank Thee for the marvelous deliverance of our fathers, and the glorious victory won by Thy help in the days of Mattathias, the priest, and his sons. The tyranny of the Syrians had threatened to make Israel forsake Thy law and renounce Thy truth. Then in the fullness of Thy mercy didst Thou aid them in their distress, fight their battles, and give victory to the feeble over the strong, to the few over the many, to the righteous over the wicked, to those who obeyed Thy word over those who assailed truth and virtue. Israel, thy people, was saved, and restored to freedom and independence. Thy children re-entered Thy temple, cleansed its halls, purified the sanctuary, illuminated it, and instituted these days of dedication as days of thanksgiving and praise to Thee. In the same way, O our Father, thy help has never been wanting to Israel whenever men arose against them and sought their destruction. Hasten the day, O God, when all hatred, all malice and prejudice shall vanish from the earth. Let all men recognize that in thine eyes, O Heavenly Father, all thy children are alike so that side by side all may labor together in love, united by a common faith in Thee. AMEN.

For Purim.

We give thanks to Thee, O Guardian of Israel, for the aid which Thou didst bestow upon our people in the days of Mordecai and Esther, at the time when the malignity of Haman threatened with destruction all the Israelites of the great Persian empire. Royal messengers had already sped throughout all its provinces, carrying the decree to slay all the children of Thy people. The day had been fixed on which the cruel counselor was to satisfy his revenge in a deluge of blood. Then by Thy might the schemes of the enemy were foiled and Thou didst thrust him into the snare which he had laid for the guiltless. In the same way, O our Father, Thy help has never been wanting to Israel whenever men arose against him and sought his destruction. Hasten the day, O God, when all hatred, all malice and prejudice shall vanish from the earth. Let all men recognize that in Thine eyes, O Heavenly Father, all Thy children are alike so that side by side all may labor together in love, united by a common faith in Thee. AMEN.

Hallelujah!

[*The School will be seated.*]

Lighting the 'Hanukkah-Candles, accompanied by appropriate Recitations.

Hymn No. 71.

Addresses, Recitations, or other Exercises.

Patriotic Hymn.

CONCLUSION.

[*The school will stand and read in unison:*]

𝔉rom age to age we give thanks to thee and tell thy praise, for our lives yielded into thy hands, for our souls entrusted to thy care, for thy marvelous works, thy wonders and boundless goodness, which thou unfoldest over us at all times, evening, morning and noon. We bless thee, the All-good, whose mercy is boundless, whose grace is infinite; our hopes are in thee forever. AMEN.

May the Lord bless us and keep us.
The Lord our God be with us as he has been with our fathers.
May the Lord let his light shine upon us and be gracious to us.
The Lord will give strength unto his people.
May the Lord lift up the light of his countenance upon us and bless us with peace.

Responsive Readings.

I.
Morning Prayer.
(Psalm 5.)

Give ear to my words, O Lord; have regard to my prayer.

Listen to the voice of my supplication, my King and my God.

In the morning will I address my prayer to thee, and look for help.

For thou art not a God that hath pleasure in wickedness;

The unrighteous man shalt not dwell with thee; the haughty shall not stand in thy sight;

Thou hatest all that do iniquity.

Thou punishest them that speak falsehood; the man of blood and deceit the Lord abhorreth.

But I, through thy great goodness, will come to thy house;

In the fear of thee will I worship at thy holy temple.

Lead me, O Lord! in thy righteousness make thy path straight before me!

Let all that put their trust in thee rejoice; because thou defendest them;

Let them that love thy name be joyful in thee!

For thou, O Lord, dost bless the righteous;

With favor dost thou encompass him, as with a shield.

II.
Acceptable Worship.
(Psalm 15.)

Lord, who shall abide at thy tabernacle? who shall dwell upon thy holy hill?

He that walketh uprightly, and doeth righteousness, and speaketh the truth from his heart;

[To give greater variety and additional material for arranging short services for the opening or closing of the school, or for the home circle, this selection of responsive readings is offered. The order of service may be in this manner: Hymn; Responsive Reading; Musical Response from one of the previous services; Prayer, either voluntary, or selected from those offered on pages 174-175; Hymn; Scripture Reading, or Address.]

He that slandereth not with his tongue, that doeth no injury to his friend,
And uttereth no reproach against his neighbor;
In whose eyes a vile person is contemned, but who honoreth them that fear the Lord;
Who sweareth to his own hurt, and changeth not;
He that lendeth not his money upon usury, and taketh not a bribe against the innocent:
He that doeth these things shall never be moved.

III.
The Dignity of Man.
(Psalm 8.)

O Eternal, our God! how excellent is thy name in all the earth! Thou hast set thy glory above the heavens.

Out of the mouths of children hast thou founded thy might, to put thy adversaries to shame, and to silence the enemy.

When I consider thy heavens, the work of thy hands, the moon and the stars which thou hast established:

What is man, that thou art mindful of him, and the son of man that thou carest for him?

Yet thou hast made him little lower than God; thou hast crowned him with glory and honor.

Thou hast given him dominion over the works of thy hands; thou hast put all things under his feet—

All sheep and cattle, yea, and the beasts of the forest;

The birds of the air, and the fishes of the sea, and whatever passeth through the paths of the deep.

O Eternal, our God, how excellent is thy name in all the earth!

IV.
God's Eternal Truth.
(Psalm 89.)

I will sing of the mercies of the Lord forever; I will make known thy faithfulness to all generations!

For I know that thy mercy endureth forever; thou hast established thy truth like the heavens.

The heavens shall praise thy wonders, O Lord! and the assembly of the holy ones thy truth!

Who in the heavens can be compared to the Lord? who is like the Eternal among the mighty?

O Lord, God of hosts! who is mighty like thee, and thy faithfulness is around about thee.

Thou rulest the raging of the sea; when the waves thereof rise, thou stillest them!

The heavens are thine; thine also is the earth; the world and all that is therein, thou didst found them.

Thine is a mighty arm; strong is thy hand, and high thy right hand.

Justice and equity are the foundation of thy throne: mercy and truth go before thy face.

Happy the people that know thy law! they walk, O Lord, in the light of thy countenance.

In thy name they daily rejoice, and in thy righteousness they glory!

For thou art the glory of their strength; yea, through thy favor we are exalted.

V.
The Praise of God.
(Psalm 146.)

Praise ye the Lord! praise the Lord, my soul!

I will praise the Lord, as long as I live; I will sing praises to my God, while I have my being.

Put not your trust in princes, in the son of man, in whom there is no help!

His breath goeth forth; he returneth to the dust; in that very day his plans perish.

Happy is he that hath the God of Jacob for his help; whose hope is in the Lord his God;

Who made heaven and earth, the sea, and all that is therein; who keepeth truth forever;

Who executeth judgment for the oppressed; who giveth food to the hungry.

The Lord setteth free the prisoners; the Lord openeth the eyes of the blind;

The Lord raiseth up them that are bowed down; the Lord loveth the righteous.

The Lord preserveth the strangers; he relieveth the fatherless and the widow.

The Lord shall reign forever; thy God, O Zion! to all generations! Hallelujah!

VI.
The Ordinances of God.
(Psalm 147.)

Praise ye the Lord! for it is good to sing praise to our God;

For it is pleasant, and praise is becoming.

He healeth the broken in heart, and bindeth up their wounds.

He counteth the number of the stars; he calleth them all by their names.

Great is our Lord, and mighty in power; his wisdom is infinite.

The Lord lifteth up the lowly; he casteth the wicked down to the ground.

Sing to the Lord with thanksgiving; sing praises upon the harp to our God!

Who covereth the heavens with clouds, who prepareth rain for the earth.

Who causeth grass to grow upon the mountains.

He giveth to the cattle their food, and to the young ravens, when they cry.

He delighteth not in the strength of the horse, he taketh not pleasure in the force of a man.

The Lord taketh pleasure in those who fear him, in those who trust in his mercy.

Praise the Lord, O Jerusalem! praise thy God, O Zion!

For he hath strengthened the bars of thy gates; he hath blessed thy children within thee.

He maketh peace in thy borders, and satisfieth thee with the finest of the wheat.

He sendeth forth his command to the earth; his word runneth swiftly.

He giveth snow like wool, and scattereth the hoar-frost like ashes.

He casteth forth his ice like morsels; who can stand before his cold?

He sendeth forth his word, and melteth them; he causeth his wind to blow, and the waters flow.

He publisheth his word to Jacob, his statutes and laws to Israel.

He hath dealt in this manner with no other nation; and, as for his ordinances, they have not known them. Hallelujah!

VII.
The Lesson of Life.
(Psalm 34.)

I will bless the Lord at all times; his praise shall continually be in my mouth.

In the Lord doth my soul boast; let the afflicted hear, and rejoice!

O magnify the Lord with me, and let us exalt his name together!

I sought the Lord, and he heard me, and delivered me from my fears.

Look up to him, and ye shall have light; your faces shall never be ashamed.

This afflicted man cried, and the Lord heard, and saved him from all his troubles.

The angels of the Lord encamp around those who fear him, and deliver them.

O taste, and see how good is the Lord! happy the man who trusteth in him!

O fear the Lord, ye his servants! for to those who fear him there shall be no want.

Come, ye children, hearken to me! I will teach you the fear of the Lord.

Who is he that loveth life, and desireth many days, in which he may see good?

Guard well thy tongue from evil, and thy lips from speaking guile.

Depart from evil, and do good: seek peace, and pursue it!

The eyes of the Lord are upon the righteous, and his ears are open to their cry.

The Lord is near to them that are of a broken heart, and saveth such as are of a contrite spirit.

Many are the afflictious of the righteous: but the Lord delivereth him from them all.

The Lord redeemeth the life of his servants, and none that put their trust in him will suffer of it.

VIII.
Steadfastness in the Law.
(Psalm 119.)

Teach me, O Lord, the way of thy statutes, and I shall keep it unto the end.

Open thou my eyes, that I may behold wonderful things out of thy law.

Give me understanding that I shall keep thy law, yea, I shall keep it with my whole heart.

Make me go in the path of thy commandments, for therein is my desire.

Turn away my eyes from beholding vanity, and quicken thou me in thy way.

Thy hands have made me and fashioned me; give me understanding that I may learn thy commandments.

Let thy tender mercies come unto me, that I may live; for thy law is my delight.

Order my footsteps in thy word, and let not any sin have dominion over me.

O Lord! thy word endureth forever, thy truth remaineth from generation to generation.

Thy word is a lamp unto my feet, and a light unto my path; it giveth understanding to the simple.

Thy testimonies are wonderful, therefore doth my soul keep them.

Thy righteousness is an everlasting righteousness, and thy law is the truth.

Let my prayer come before thee, O Lord! give me understanding according to thy word.

My lips shall speak thy praise, when thou hast taught me thy statutes.

I have longed for thy salvation, O Lord, and in thy law is my glory.

The righteousness of thy testimonies is everlasting; Oh, grant me understanding and I shall live.

Thy testimonies are my heritage forever; quicken me, O Lord! according to thy lovingkindness.

IX.
The Kingdom of God.
(Psalm 145.)

I will extol thee, my God, O King, I will bless thy name forever and ever.

Every day will I bless thee, and I will praise thy name forever.

Great is the Lord and highly to be praised; his greatness is unsearchable.

One generation shall praise thy works to another, and shall declare thy mighty deeds.

I will speak of the glorious honor of thy majesty, and of thy wonderful works.

Men shall speak of the might of thy wonderful deeds, and I will declare thy greatness.

They shall remember thy great goodness, and sing of thy righteousness.

The Lord is gracious and full of compassion, slow to anger and rich in mercy.

The Lord is good to all, and his tender mercies are over all his works.

All thy works praise thee, O God, and thy holy ones bless thee.

They proclaim the glory of thy kingdom, and speak of thy power.

Thy kingdom is an everlasting kingdom, and thy dominion endureth forever.

The Lord upholdeth the falling, and uplifteth those who are bowed down.

The eyes of all wait upon thee, and thou givest them their food in due season.

Thou openest thy hand and satisfiest the desire of every living being.

The Lord is righteous in all his ways, and merciful in all his works.

The Lord is near to all who call upon him, who call upon him in truth.

He fulfilleth the desire of those that fear him; he will hear their cry and save them.

My mouth shall praise the Lord; and let all flesh bless his holy name forever and ever.

Let us praise the Lord henceforth and forever. Hallelujah!

X.
Victory.
(Psalms 44 and 46.)

O God! we have heard with our ears, our fathers have told us, what deeds thou didst in their days, in the days of old.

Thou didst subdue the nations, and cause our fathers to flourish.

For not by their own swords did they gain possession of the land,

Nor did their own arms give them victory; but thy right hand, and thy arm, and the light of thy countenance.

Thou art my King, O God! Through thee we may triumph over our enemies;

In God will we glory continually; yea, we will praise thy name forever!

God is our refuge and strength; an ever-present help in trouble.

Therefore will we not fear, though the earth be changed;

Though the mountains tremble in heart of the sea;

Though its waters roar and be troubled, and the mountains shake with the swelling thereof.

A river with its streams shall make glad the city God, the holy dwelling-place of the Most High.

God is in the midst of her; she shall not be moved; God will help her, and that full early.

The nations raged; kingdoms were moved; he uttered his voice, the earth melted.

The Lord of hosts is with us; the God of Jacob is our refuge.

Come, behold the doings of the Lord; what desolations he hath made in the earth!

He causeth wars to cease to the end of the earth; he hath broken the bow, and snapped the spear asunder, and burned the chariots in fire.

The Lord of hosts is with us; the God of Jacob is our refuge.

XI.
Trust in God.

(Psalms 23, 16 and 121.)

The Lord is my shepherd; I shall not want.

He maketh me lie down in green pastures; he leadeth me beside the still waters.

He reviveth my soul; he leadeth me in paths of safety, for his name's sake.

When I walk through the valley of the shadow of death I fear no evil;

For thou art with me; thy stay and thy staff, they comfort me.

Thou preparest a table before me in the presence of my enemies.

Thou annointest my head with oil; my cup runneth over.

Surely goodness and mercy shall follow me all the days of my life, and I shall dwell in the house of the Lord forever.

My portion hath fallen to me in pleasant places; yea, I have a goodly inheritance.

I will bless the Lord, who careth for me; yea, in the night my heart admonisheth me.

I set the Lord before me at all time; since he is at my right hand, I shall not fall.

Therefore my heart is glad, and my spirit rejoiceth; yea, my flesh dwelleth in security.

I lift up my eyes to the hills; whence cometh my help?

My help cometh from the Lord, who made heaven and earth.

He will not suffer thy foot to stumble; thy guardian doth not slumber.

Behold, the guardian of Israel doth neither slumber nor sleep.

The Lord is thy guardian; the Lord is thy shade at thy right hand.

The sun shall not smite thee by day, nor the moon by night.

The Lord will preserve thee from all evil; he will preserve thy life.

The Lord will preserve thy going out and thy coming in, from this time forth forever.

XII.

The Praise of Wisdom.

(Proverbs.)

Happy the man who findeth wisdom; yea, the man who getteth understanding!

For the profit thereof is greater than that of silver, and the gain thereof than that of fine gold.

More precious is she than pearls, and none of thy jewels is to be compared with her.

Length of days is in her right hand, in her left hand are riches and honor.

Her ways are ways of pleasantness, and all her paths are peace.

    She is a tree of life to them that lay hold of her, and happy is everyone who clings to her.

Let not kindness and truth forsake thee; bind them around thy neck, write them upon the tablets of thy heart:

    Then shalt thou find favor and good success in the sight of God and man.

Be not wise in thine own eyes; fear the Lord, and depart from evil.

    Withhold not kindness from those who need it, when it is in the power of thy hand to do it.

His own iniquities shall ensnare the wicked; yea he shall be held fast by the cords of his own sins.

    But the path of the righteous is as the light of dawn, which groweth brighter and brighter unto the perfect day.

The way of the wicked is as thick darkness; they know not at what they stumble.

    More than anything which thou watchest, watch the heart; for from it are the issues of life.

My son, despise not the correction of the Lord, nor be impatient under his chastisement!

    For whom the Lord loveth he chasteneth, even as a father the son in whom he delighteth.

Riches do not profit in the day of wrath; but righteousness delivereth from death.

    In the path of righteousness is life, and in her pathway there is no death.

Prayer.

    Eternal, our God, may it be thy will to lead us in thy ways, that thy name be honored and Israel blessed through our actions. May we walk according to the precepts of thy law, then shall we never fall into temptation, sin and shame. May our better nature always prompt us to do good with a willing heart, and to faithfully discharge the duties of life. Gird us with strength to rule over our spirit according to thy will. Help us, O Father, that our actions may be always such as to win us love and favor in thine eyes, and in the eyes of our fellow men; for thou alone bestowest mercy and grace upon the children of men, and aidest with thy love all who honor thee through a virtuous and upright life. AMEN.

PRAYERS.

I.

Praise be to thee, our Father, for the day of light and the night's stillness, for the earth's beauty and the heavens of the sun and stars, for our beloved on the earth, for the thought of thee in our hearts, for the knowledge of duty, and for immortal life.

II.

Our God and Father, these words which thou hast commanded us this day—let them be in our hearts. Let us talk of them in our dwellings. When we lie down, and when we arise, and when we walk by the way, let them be a sign to our eyes and a path to our feet.

III.

Father of truth, around us and in us art thou—Eternal Light which illumines our darkness. Give us light to search thy teachings without ceasing, Lord, to behold in thy laws the way of our feet. Blessed be thou Father Eternal, who hast given us thy teachings and set thy law within us.

IV.

Blessed be thy name, O Eternal, Giver and Guardian of life, by whom is the earth and all that is therein, the peace of the evening, the sleep of the night, the awaking of the morning in strength, and the labor of the day! True praise be within us unto thee, O Lord!

V.

Holy Eternal One, thou hast shown us what is good and what thou dost require of us, to do justly, to love mercy, and to walk humbly with God. Great peace have they who love thy law, and nothing can offend them.

VI.

The law of the Lord is perfect, giving life to the soul. The precepts of the Lord are sure, giving wisdom to the simple. Let the words of my mouth and the meditations of my heart be acceptable in thy sight, O Lord, my Strength and my Deliverer.

VII.

It is our duty to render praise and thanksgiving unto the Creator of heaven and earth, who delivered us from the darkness of false belief and revealed to us the light of his truth. He is our God, there is none besides.

VIII.

Extolled and hallowed be the great name of God throughout the world, which he has created according to his will. His name is the Infinite, Eternal, All-holy, All-merciful, who reneweth daily in lovingkindness the work of creation.

IX.

Our God, God of our fathers, may thy love rule over all thy works and the reverence for thee fill the hearts of all thy creatures; that all the children of men bow before thee in humility, and unite to do thy will with an upright heart, that they may all proclaim that thine is the kingdom, the power and the majesty, and that thy name is exalted above all.

X.

Praise be to thee, Father of all, who callest in the evening and openest the gates of the morning. Thou changest times and seasons; thou settest stars in their watches; thou leadest forth the day. In this day, which thou makest for us, may we reverence thy holy law within us, that we be not put to shame by our deeds.

XI.

Our Heavenly Father, thy presence makes heaven everywhere. We bless thee for this beautiful earth and for the years thou hast given us in it. Thou hast filled the spring-time with flowers, the summer with corn and fruit; and thou hast fed our bodies with plenty and our minds with truth. In winter thou hast clothed the earth with snow like wool, and thou hast kept our bodies warm and our hearts glad. Thou hast waked us and led us forth refreshed, when thou hast spread the morning upon the mountains; when thou hast called forth the darkness and set the stars in their places; thou hast poured sleep on our eyelids and overshadowed us with thy wings in the night. Like as a father pitieth his children, thou hast pitied us and watched over us. We cannot number thy blessings; we cannot declare thy love. For all thy lovingkindness we bless thee and praise thee, our Father. We ask not anything but to trust thee who hast made the past so full of joy. We trust and bless thee forever and ever. AMEN.

Hebrew Responses and Hymns.

For New Year and Day of Atonement.
(Traditional.)

No. 20. Adon Olom.

En kelohenu. Concluded.

Mah-tovu. Concluded.

God My King.

Psalm CXLV. (Arranged from BEETHOVEN.)

1. God, my King, Thy might confessing, Ev - er will I bless Thy name;
2. They shall talk of all Thy glo - ry, On Thy might and great-ness dwell;
3. Full of kind-ness and com-pas-sion, Slow to an - ger, vast in love,

Day by day Thy throne ad-dressing, Still will I Thy praise proclaim.
Speak of Thy dread acts in sto - ry, And Thy deeds of won-der tell.
God is good to all cre - a - tion; All His works His goodness prove.

Hon - or great our King be - fit-teth; Who His maj - es - ty can reach?
Nor shall fall from memory's treasure, Works of love and mer - cy wrought—
All Thy works O God, shall bless Thee, All cre - a - tion Thou a - dore;

Age to age His works transmitteth, Age to age His power shall teach,
Works of love sur - pass-ing meas-ure, Works of mer - cy pass - ing thought.
Kings and rul - ers shall con-fess Thee And pro-claim Thy sovereign power.

Who is Like Thee?

(P. C. Lutkin.)

1. Who is like Thee, O U-ni-ver-sal Lord! Who dare Thy praise and glo-ry share? Who is in heav'n, Most High, like Thee a-dored? Who can on earth with Thee com-pare? Thou art the One true God a-lone, And firm-ly found-ed is Thy throne.
2. Thy ten-der love em-brac-es all man-kind, As chil-dren all by Thee are blest; Re-pent-ant sin-ners with Thee mer-cy find, Thy hand up-hold-eth the op-prest; All worlds at-test Thy pow'r sub-lime, Thy glo-ry shines in ev-'ry clime.
3. And to Thy might and love is joined in Thee The high-est wis-dom's liv-ing spring; What-e'er to us is deep-est mys-ter-y, Is clear to Thee, our Lord and King. O God of wis-dom, love and might, We wor-ship Thee, E-ter-nal Light.

Who is Like Thee?
Second tune. (MENDELSSOHN.)

1. Who is like Thee, O U-ni-ver-sal Lord! Who dare Thy praise and glo-ry share? Who is in heav'n, Most High, like Thee a-dored? Who can on earth with Thee com-pare? Thou art the One true God a-lone, And firm-ly found-ed is Thy throne.

2. Thy ten-der love em-braces all man-kind, As chil-dren all by Thee are blest; Re-pen-tant sin-ners with Thee mercy find, Thy hand up-hold-eth the op-prest; All worlds at-test Thy pow'r sub-lime, Thy glo-ry shines in ev-'ry clime.

3. And to Thy might and love is joined in Thee The high-est wis-dom's liv-ing spring; What-e'er to us is deep-est mys-ter-y, Is clear to Thee, our Lord and King. O God of wis-dom, love and might, We wor-ship Thee, E-ter-nal Light.

The Offering

210

Morning Hymn.

211

Faith.

1. Sum - mer suns are glow - ing O - ver land and sea,
   Hap - py light is flow - ing Boun - ti - ful and free.
   Ev - 'ry thing re - joic - es In the mel - low rays,
   All earth's thousand voic - es Swell the psalm of praise.

2. God's free mer - cy stream - eth O - ver all the world,
   And His ban - ner gleam - eth Ev - 'ry-where un - furled,
   Broad and deep and glo - rious As the heav'ns a - bove,
   Shines in night vic - to - rious His e - ter - nal love.

3. We will nev - er doubt Thee Though Thou veil Thy light;
   Life is dark with - out Thee; Death with Thee is bright
   Light of light! shine o'er us On our pil - grim way,
   Go Thou still be - fore us To the end - less day.

God is All.

1. Blest be Thou, O God of Is-rael, Thou, our Fa-ther and our God;
2. Rich-es come of Thee and hon-or, Pow'r and might to Thee be-long;

Bless Thy maj-es-ty for ev-er; Ev-er be Thy name a-dored.
Thine it is to make us pros-per, On-ly Thine to make us strong.

Thine O Lord are pow'r and greatness; Glo-ry, vic-t'ry are Thine own;
Lord, to Thee, thou God of mer-cy; Hymns of grat-i-tude we raise;

All is Thine in earth and heav-en, O-ver all Thy bound-less throne.
To Thy name for-ev-er glo-rious, Ev-er we ad-dress our praise.

Holy Ground.

ARR. from BEETHOVEN.

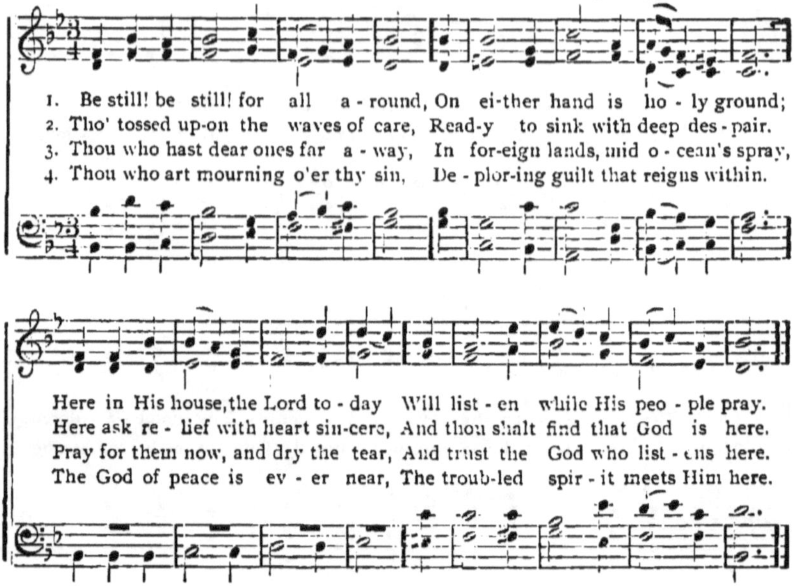

1. Be still! be still! for all a-round, On ei-ther hand is ho-ly ground;
2. Tho' tossed up-on the waves of care, Read-y to sink with deep des-pair.
3. Thou who hast dear ones far a-way, In for-eign lands, mid o-cean's spray,
4. Thou who art mourning o'er thy sin, De-plor-ing guilt that reigns within.

Here in His house, the Lord to-day Will list-en while His peo-ple pray.
Here ask re-lief with heart sin-cere, And thou shalt find that God is here.
Pray for them now, and dry the tear, And trust the God who list-ens here.
The God of peace is ev-er near, The troub-led spir-it meets Him here.

Evening Song.

W. A. MOZART.

1. Gen-tly the twi-light hours are near-ing, Like an-gels fair to men ap-
2. Blest is that pow'r from heav'n decend-ing, Its ho-ly peace to all hearts
3. When evening comes in sun-set splen-dor, When weary hearts grow soft and

pearing. The peaceful hours their mag-ic throw On wea-ry
lending, Save to that one whose work has been To pass the
ten-der, How dear thy sway, how swift thy flight, Thou peaceful,

214

spir - its here be - low, On wea-ry spir - its here be - low.
fleet - ing hours in sin, To pass the fleet - ing hours in sin.
ho - ly, star - lit night, Thou peaceful, ho - ly, star - lit night.

Morning Anthem.

With simplicity and dignity. (J. H. ROLLE.)

1. Praise the Lord! Praise the Lord! The morn - ing
2. Praise the Lord! Praise the Lord! In ver - - nal
3. Praise the Lord! Praise the Lord! From out their

sun a - wakes .... the fields from night - ly rest, And the
beau - ty prais - es him the flor - - al year, In the
dens the wild ..... beasts loud-ly roar their praise, O my

whole cre - a - tion's gladness streams .. Re - born in - to our breast.
skies, and in the leaf - y bow'rs, .. The bird's glad song we hear.
soul! more loudly still to God .... Thy grate-ful trib - ute raise.

From the "Carol," by per. The John Church Co.

Faith and Hope.

Old German Melody.

1. The world may change from old to new, From new to old a-gain,
Yet hope and faith, for-ev-er true, With-in man's heart re-main.
The dreams that bless the wea-ry soul, The strug-gles of the strong,
Are steps to-ward some hap-py goal, The sto-ry of hope's song.

2. Hope leads the child to plant the flow'r, The man to sow the seed;
Nor leaves ful-fil-ment to the hour, But prompts a-gain to deed;
And ere up-on the old man's dust The grass is seen to wave,
We look thro' fall-ing tears to trust Hope's sun-shine in the grave.

3. Oh, no! it is no flat-t'ring lure, No fan-cy weak or fond,
When hope would bid us rest se-cure In the bet-ter life be-yond.
Nor love, nor shame, nor grief, nor sin, His prom-ise may gain-say;
The voice di-vine hath spoke with-in, And God can-not be-tray.

The Lord Almighty Reigneth.

218

www.ingramcontent.com/pod-product-compliance
Lightning Source LLC
Chambersburg PA
CBHW031817230426
43669CB00009B/1170